PIMLICO

442

BRUNELLESCHI'S DOME

Ross King is the author of two novels, *Domino* and *Ex-Libris*, which have been translated into seven languages. He lives near Oxford.

BRUNELLESCHI'S DOME

The Story of the Great Cathedral in Florence

ROSS KING

PIMLICO

Published by Pimlico 2001

2 4 6 8 10 9 7 5 3 1

First published in Great Britain by
Chatto & Windus 2000
Pimlico edition 2001

Pimlico
Random House, 20 Vauxhall Bridge Road,
London SW1V 2SA

Random House Australia (Pty) Limited
20 Alfred Street, Milsons Point, Sydney,
New South Wales 2061, Australia

Random House New Zealand Limited
18 Poland Road, Glenfield,
Auckland 10, New Zealand

Random House (Pty) Limited
Endulini, 5A Jubilee Road, Parktown 2193, South Africa

Random House Group Limited Reg. No. 954009
www.randomhouse.co.uk

A CIP catalogue record for this book
is available from the British Library

ISBN 0-7126-6480-7

Papers used by Random House are natural,
recyclable products made from wood grown in sustainable forests.
The manufacturing processes conform to the environmental
regulations of the country of origin

Printed and bound in Great Britain by
Biddles Ltd, Guildford

For Mark Asquith and Anne-Marie Rigard

Acknowledgements

My thanks to everyone who assisted with the research and writing of this book. I am indebted to Alta Macadam for reading the manuscript and sharing with me her encyclopaedic knowledge of Florence, and to Sir Jack Zunz for his expertise in structural engineering and his understanding of the finer points of Brunelleschi's technological achievement. A number of other people also read the manuscript in draft form and offered valuable advice: Mark Asquith, Ronald Jonkers, Sophie Oxenham, Anne-Marie Rigard and Amir Ramezani. For help with translations I am grateful to Cristiana Papi and to my sister Maureen King. Thanks also to Maureen for tracking down a number of important periodical articles that would otherwise have been inaccessible to me. Sarah Challis executed diagrams for the text, while Margaret Duffy and Richard Mabey provided information in response to my queries. During the course of my research I was assisted on numerous occasions by the staffs of the British Library, the Bodleian Library, the London Library and the Oxford University Engineering Science Library.

I also wish to thank my editors, Rebecca Carter and Roger Cazalet, both of whom saved me from errors in presentation and infelicities of style; my agent, Christopher Sinclair-Stevenson, whose steadfast support for the project was vital at every stage; and my German editor, Karl-Heinz Bittel, whose support has likewise kept the book afloat. Finally, I must record my thanks to the two people to whom the book is dedicated, Mark Asquith and Anne-Marie Rigard. I will always be grateful for their hospitality in London and companionship in Florence, but above all for their constant friendship.

Contents

Illustrations

BLACK AND WHITE ILLUSTRATIONS

COLOUR PLATES

The author and publisher are grateful for permission to reproduce illustrations in this book, and to Sarah Challis and Eugenio Battisti for their diagrams.

A More Beautiful and Honourable Temple

ON THE NINETEENTH OF AUGUST 1418 a competition was announced in Florence, where the city's magnificent new cathedral, Santa Maria del Fiore, had been under construction for more than a century:

> *Whoever desires to make any model or design for the vaulting of the main Dome of the Cathedral under construction by the Opera del Duomo — for armature, scaffold or other thing, or any lifting device pertaining to the construction and perfection of said cupola or vault — shall do so before the end of the month of September. If the model be used he shall be entitled to a payment of 200 gold Florins.*

Two hundred florins was a good deal of money — more than a skilled craftsman could earn in two years of work — and so the competition attracted the attention of carpenters, masons and cabinet-makers from all across Tuscany. They had six weeks to build their models, draw their designs, or simply make suggestions how the dome of the cathedral might be built. Their proposals were intended to solve a variety of problems, including how a temporary wooden support network could be constructed to hold the dome's masonry in place, and how sandstone and marble blocks each weighing several tons might be raised to its top. The Opera del Duomo — the office of works in charge of the cathedral — reassured all prospective competitors that their efforts would receive 'a friendly and trustworthy audience'.

Already at work on the building site, which sprawled through the heart of Florence, were scores of other craftsmen: carters, bricklayers, lead-beaters, even cooks and men whose job it was to sell wine to the workers on their lunch breaks. From the piazza surrounding the cathedral the men could be seen carting bags of sand and lime, or else clambering about on wooden scaffolds and wickerwork platforms that rose above the neighbouring rooftops like a great, untidy bird's nest. Nearby, a forge for repairing their tools belched clouds of black smoke into the sky, and from dawn to dusk the air rang with the blows of the blacksmith's hammer and with the rumble of ox-carts and the shouting of orders.

Florence in the early 1400s still retained a rural aspect. Wheatfields, orchards and vineyards could be found inside its walls, while flocks of sheep were driven bleating through the streets to the market near the Baptistery of San Giovanni. But the city also had a population of 50,000, roughly the same as London's, and the new cathedral was intended to reflect its importance as a large and powerful mercantile city. Florence had become one of the most prosperous cities in Europe. Much of its wealth came from the wool industry started by the Umiliati monks soon after their arrival in the city in 1239. Bales of English wool – the finest in the world – were brought from monasteries in the Cotswolds to be washed in the River Arno, combed, spun into yarn, woven on wooden looms, then dyed beautiful colours: vermilion, made from cinnabar gathered on the shores of the Red Sea, or a brilliant yellow procured from the crocuses growing in meadows near the hilltop town of San Gimignano. The result was the most expensive and most sought-after cloth in Europe.

Because of this prosperity, Florence had undergone a building boom during the 1300s the like of which had not been seen in Italy since the time of the Ancient Romans. Quarries of golden-brown sandstone were opened inside the city walls; sand from the River Arno, dredged and filtered after every flood, was used in the making of mortar, and gravel was harvested from the riverbed to fill in the walls of the dozens of new buildings that had begun springing up all over the city. These included churches, monasteries and private palaces, as well as monumental structures such as a new ring of defensive walls to protect the city from invaders. Standing twenty feet high and running five miles in circumference, these fortifications, not finished until 1340, took more than fifty years to build. An imposing new town hall, the Palazzo Vecchio, had also been constructed, complete with a bell tower that stood more than three hundred feet high. Another impressive tower was the cathedral's 280-foot campanile, with its bas-reliefs and multicoloured encrustations of marble. Designed by the painter Giotto, it had been completed in 1359, after more than two decades of work.

Yet by 1418 what was by far the grandest building project in Florence had still to be completed. A replacement for the ancient and dilapidated church of Santa Reparata, the new cathedral of Santa Maria del Fiore was intended to be one of the largest in Christendom. Entire forests had been requisitioned to provide timber for it, and huge slabs of marble were being transported along the Arno on flotillas of boats. From the outset its construction had as much to do with civic pride as religious faith: the cathedral was to be built, the Commune of Florence had stipulated, with the greatest lavishness and magnificence possible, and once completed it was to be 'a more beautiful and honourable temple than any in any other party of Tuscany'. But it was clear that the builders faced major obstacles, and the closer the cathedral came to completion, the more difficult their task would become.

The way forward should have been clear enough. For the past fifty years the south aisle of the unfinished cathedral had housed a 30-foot-long scale model of the structure, in effect an artist's impression of what the cathedral should look like once finished. The problem was that the model included an enormous dome – a dome that, if built, would be the highest and widest vault ever raised. And for fifty years it had been obvious that no one in Florence – or anywhere in Italy, for that matter – had any clear idea how to construct it. The unbuilt dome of Santa Maria del Fiore had therefore become the greatest architectural puzzle of the age. Many experts considered its erection an impossible feat. Even the original planners of the dome had been unable to advise how their project might be completed: they merely expressed a touching faith that at some point in the future God might provide a solution and that architects with a more advanced knowledge would be found.

The foundation stone for the new cathedral had been laid in 1296. The designer and original architect was a master mason named Arnolfo di Cambio, the builder of both the Palazzo Vecchio and the city's massive new fortifications. Although Arnolfo died soon after construction began, the masons forged on, and over the next few decades a whole section of Florence was razed to make way for the new building. Santa Reparata and another ancient church, San Michele Visdomini, were both demolished and the inhabitants of the surrounding district were displaced from their homes. Not only the living were evicted: in order to open a piazza in front of the church, the bones of long-dead Florentines were exhumed from their graves surrounding the Baptistery of San Giovanni, which stood a few feet to the west of the building site. In 1339 one of the streets south of the cathedral, the Corso degli Adamari (now the Via dei Calzaiuoli) was lowered so that the cathedral's height should appear even more impressive to anyone approaching from that direction.

But as Santa Maria del Fiore grew steadily larger, Florence was shrinking. In the autumn of 1347 the Genoese fleet returned to Italy carrying in its holds not only spices from India but also the Asian black rat, carrier of the Black Death. As much as four-fifths of the population of Florence were to die over the next twelve months, so depopulating the city that Tartar and Circassian slaves were imported to ease the labour shortages. As late as 1355, therefore, nothing existed of the cathedral except for the façade and the walls of the nave. The interior of the church lay open to the elements, like a ruin, and the foundations for the unbuilt east end had been exposed for so long that one of the streets east of the cathedral was known as Lungo di Fondamenti, or 'Along the Founda-tions'.

Over the next decade, however, as the city gradually recovered, work on

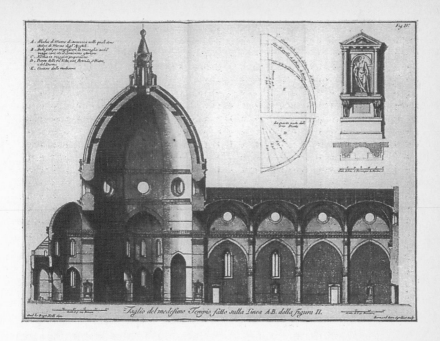

1. A section drawing of Santa Maria del Fiore by Giovanni Battista Nelli.

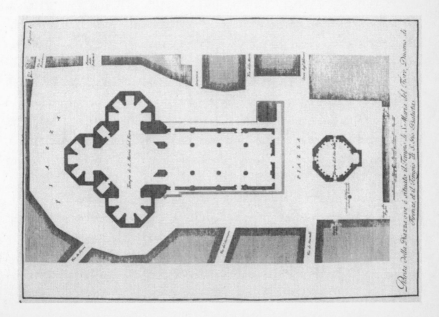

2. A ground plan of the cathedral showing the three tribunes, with their chapels, around the dome's octagon. On the right, in the piazza, is the Baptistery.

the cathedral accelerated, and by 1366 the nave had been vaulted and the east end of the church, which included the dome, was ready to be planned. Arnolfo di Cambio had undoubtedly envisioned a dome for the church, but there is no surviving evidence of his original design: some time in the fourteenth century his model of the cathedral collapsed under its own weight – an ominous sign – and was subsequently lost or demolished. But excavations during the 1970s uncovered the foundations for a dome that was intended to have a span of 62 *braccia*, or 119 feet (a Florentine *braccia* being 23 inches, roughly the length of a man's arm).[1] With this diameter the cupola of Santa Maria del Fiore would have exceeded by some twelve feet the span of the dome of the world's most spectacular church, Santa Sophia in Constantinople, which had been built 900 years earlier by the Emperor Justinian.

Since the 1330s responsibility for building and funding the cathedral had been in the hands of Florence's largest, wealthiest and most powerful guild, the Wool Merchants, who administered the Opera del Duomo. None of the wardens running the Opera knew the first thing about building churches: their business was wool, not architecture. It therefore fell to them to appoint someone who did understand the craft, an architect-in-chief, or *capomaestro*, who would create the models and designs for the cathedral and also deal with the masons and other builders involved in the actual construction. In 1366, as planning reached its crucial stage, the *capomaestro* of Santa Maria del Fiore was a man named Giovanni di Lapo Ghini. At the request of the Opera, Giovanni began building a model for the cathedral's dome. But the wardens also ordered a second model from a group of artists and masons led by another master mason, Neri di Fioravanti.[2] The fate of Santa Maria del Fiore was about to undergo a radical change.

Competition between architects was an old and honoured custom. Patrons had been making architects compete against one another for their commissions since at least 448 BC, when the Council of Athens held a public competition for the war memorial it planned to build on the Acropolis. Under these circumstances, it was normal practice for architects to produce models as a means of convincing patrons or panels of judges of the virtues of their particular designs. Made from wood, stone, brick or even clay or wax, such models allowed the patrons to visualise the dimensions and decorations of the end product much more easily than would a diagram executed on parchment. They were often large and highly detailed – so large, in fact, that in many cases patrons could walk inside to inspect the interior. The brick-and-plaster model for San Petronio in Bologna, for example, built in 1390, was 59 feet long and, therefore, a good deal larger than most houses.

Giovanni di Lapo Ghini set about building a model that was fairly traditional in style. He planned a typically Gothic structure with thin walls, tall windows and, to support the dome, external buttresses of the sort adorning so many of the churches built in France during the previous century. Buttresses were one of the prime structural features of Gothic architecture: by accommodating the thrust of the vaults transferred to them from strategic points they allowed for walls pierced by a multitude of windows to rise to spectacular heights, filling the church with heavenly light – the aspiration of all Gothic builders.

Neri di Fioravanti and his group rejected the external supports proposed by Giovanni di Lapo Ghini, however, and offered a different approach to the structure of the dome. Flying buttresses were rare in Italy, where architects regarded them as ugly and awkward makeshifts.[3] But Neri's reasons for rejecting them were probably political as much as aesthetic or structural in that they smacked of the architecture of Florence's traditional enemies: Germany, France and Milan. How the German barbarians, the Goths, had covered Europe with their clumsy and disproportional edifices would later become a popular theme with writers of the Italian Renaissance.

But if no flying buttresses were to be built, how was the dome to be supported? Neri di Fioravanti, the principal master mason in Florence, had extensive experience in vaulting, the most dangerous and difficult architectural manoeuvre. He was the man responsible for erecting the enormous 60-foot-wide vaults over the great hall of the Bargello as well as the arches of the new Ponte Vecchio after the old bridge was swept away by a flood in 1333. But his plan for the dome of Santa Maria del Fiore was far more ambitious and largely untested: he believed the dome could be prevented from buckling under its own weight not by means of external buttresses but by the incorporation of a series of stone or wooden chains that would run round the circumference, encircling the dome at the points of possible rupture in the same way that an iron hoop contains the staves of a barrel. All of the lines of stress would therefore be absorbed by the structure itself without being channelled to the ground by means of external buttresses. Unlike buttresses, moreover, these circumferential rings, buried in the dome's masonry, would be invisible. And it was this vision of a massive dome that seemed to rise heavenwards without any visible means of support that for the next half-century would both inspire and frustrate everyone involved with the project.

The wardens in the Opera del Duomo did not decide between the two models without a good deal of debate. At first Neri and his group seemed to win the day, but Giovanni succeeded in raising questions about the stability of their design. His doubts illustrate a fear that haunted architects in the Middle Ages. Today a patron who hires an engineer takes it for granted that the end product will stand, even through earthquakes and hurricanes. But in the Middle Ages and the Renaissance, before the science of statics was developed, a patron enjoyed no such assurance, and it was not uncommon for buildings to fall down soon after completion, or even during the building process itself. The bell towers in both Pisa and Bologna began to lean while still under construction because of subsidence in the underlying soil, while the vaults in the cathedrals at both Beauvais and Troyes collapsed a relatively short time after being raised. The superstitious attributed these failures to supernatural causes, but to the more knowledgeable the real culprits were the architects and builders who had made fundamental (though imperfectly understood) errors in design.

In the end Giovanni's concerns led the wardens to stipulate that, although Neri's model would be adopted, the pillars that supported the dome should be enlarged. But enlarging the pillars would create perhaps even greater problems. Their dimensions were directly related to those of the octagonal tribune, whose perimeter they would form. The foundations for an octagon of 62 *braccia* had already been begun: would this groundwork have to be undone? Even more serious, the diameter of the tribune could not be enlarged without a corresponding increase in the span of the cupola. Was it possible to build a dome with a span even larger than 62 *braccia*, still without the use of any visible supports?

These questions were addressed at the meeting in August 1367 in which the wardens opted for a dome that would be 10 *braccia* wider than the one previously planned. Three months later, in keeping with Florentine democracy – and also, perhaps, in keeping with a desire on the part of the wardens to spread the blame as widely as possible – the plan was endorsed by a referendum of Florence's citizens.

The decision to adopt Neri di Fioravanti's design represents a remarkable leap of faith. No dome approaching this span had been built since Antiquity, and with a mean diameter of 143 feet and 6 inches it would exceed that of even the Roman Pantheon, which for over a thousand years had been the world's largest dome by far. And the cupola of Santa Maria del Fiore would not only be the widest vault ever built: it would also be the highest. The walls of the cathedral were already 140 feet high, above which a tambour (or drum) on which the dome was to rest would rise another 30 feet. The purpose of this tambour was to elevate the dome – to serve, in effect, as a pedestal, raising the dome even higher above the city.[4] Vaulting for the cupola would therefore begin at an incredible height of 170 feet, much higher than any of the Gothic vaults built in France during the thirteenth century. Indeed, the highest Gothic vault ever constructed, in the Cathedral of Saint-Pierre at Beauvais, began at just under 126 feet and rose to a maximum height of 157 feet, still a good 13 feet below where the vaulting for the dome of Santa Maria del Fiore was to begin. And the choir at Beauvais spanned only 51 feet in contrast to the 143 feet proposed for the cupola in Florence. The fact that the main vaults of the choir in Saint-Pierre had collapsed in 1284, little more than a decade after completion, cannot have eased the minds of the sceptics, especially since the architects at Beauvais had made use of both iron tie rods and flying buttresses, the expedients so boldly rejected by the committee of artists and masons.

Despite all the challenges it presented, Neri di Fioravanti's model set the basic form for the dome of Santa Maria del Fiore as it would ultimately be constructed. Intriguingly, it was to consist of not one but *two* domes, with one shell fitting inside the other. This type of structure was rare, though not unique, in Western Europe.[5] Developed during the medieval period in Persia, it had become a characteristic feature of Islamic mosques and mausoleums. In such structures a tall outer shell was intended to give impressive height to the building, while the shallower inner one – which partially supported the outer dome – was more suited to the interior proportions. The outer dome also shielded the inner one from the elements, serving as a weathering skin.

Besides the double shell, the other special feature of Neri's dome was its particular shape. Unlike most previous cupolas, including the Pantheon, that of Santa Maria del Fiore was to be pointed rather than hemispherical in profile. That is, instead of describing a semicircle, its sides would curve up towards a point in the same way that Gothic arches do. This shape was known as a *quinto acuto* or 'pointed fifth'. In technical terms the dome was to be an octagonal cloister-vault composed of four interpenetrating barrel vaults. This complex structure was to create unforeseen problems for the men who began to build it fifty years later, and its construction would call for ingenious solutions.

Neri's model of the dome became an object of veneration in Florence. Standing 15 feet high and 30 feet long, it was displayed like a reliquary or shrine in one of the side aisles of the growing cathedral. Every year the cathedral's architects and wardens were obliged to place their hands on a copy of the Bible and swear an oath that they would build the church exactly as the model portrayed. Many aspiring carpenters and masons must also have walked past it on their way in and out of the cathedral, contemplating the problems of the dome's construction and dreaming of their solution. Thus when the competition to solve these difficulties was announced in the summer of 1418, more than a dozen models were submitted to the Opera by various hopefuls, some by craftsmen from as far away as Pisa and Siena.

However, of the many plans submitted, only one – a model that offered a magnificently daring and unorthodox solution to the problem of vaulting such a large space – appeared to show much promise. This model, made of brick, was built not by a carpenter or mason but by a man who would make it his life's work to solve the puzzles of the dome's construction: a goldsmith and clockmaker named Filippo Brunelleschi.

The Goldsmith of San Giovanni

IN 1418 FILIPPO BRUNELLESCHI — or 'Pippo', as he was known to everyone — was forty-one years old. He lived in the San Giovanni district of Florence, just west of the cathedral, in a large house he had inherited from his father, a prosperous and well-travelled notary named Ser Brunellesco di Lippo Lappi. Ser Brunellesco originally intended his son to follow in his footsteps, but Filippo had scant interest in a career as a civil servant, showing instead, from a young age, an uncanny talent for solving mechanical problems. No doubt his interest in machines had been sparked by the sight of the half-built cathedral that stood a short walk from the family home. Growing up in the shadow of Santa Maria del Fiore he would have seen in daily operation the treadwheel hoists and cranes that had been designed to raise blocks of marble and sandstone to the top of the building. And the mystery of how to build the dome was probably a topic of conversation in the family home: Ser Brunellesco possessed some knowledge of the subject, having been one of the citizens who in the referendum of 1367 had voted for the bold design of Neri di Fioravanti.

Although disappointed by his son's lack of desire to become a notary, Ser Brunellesco respected the boy's wishes, and when he was fifteen Filippo was apprenticed in the workshop of a family friend, a goldsmith named

Benincasa Lotti. An apprenticeship with a goldsmith was a wise and logical choice for a boy showing mechanical ingenuity. Goldsmiths were the princes among the artisans of the Middle Ages, with a large scope to explore their numerous and varied talents. They could decorate a manuscript with gold leaf, set precious stones, cast metals, work with enamel, engrave silver and fashion anything from a gold button to a shrine, reliquary or tomb. It is no coincidence that the sculptors Andrea Orcagna, Luca della Robbia and Donatello, as well as the painters Paolo Uccello, Andrea del Verrocchio, Leonardo da Vinci and Benozzo Gozzoli – some of the brightest stars in a remarkable constellation of Florentine artists and craftsmen – had all originally trained in the workshops of goldsmiths.

Despite its prestige, goldsmithing was not the most wholesome of professions. The large furnaces that were needed to melt gold, copper and bronze had to burn for days on end, even in the heat of summer, polluting the air with smoke and bringing the danger of explosions and fire. Noxious substances such as sulphur and lead were used to engrave silver, and the clay moulds in which metals were cast required supplies of both cow dung and charred ox-horn. Worse still, the workshops of most goldsmiths were found in Florence's most notorious slum, Santa Croce, a marshy and flood-prone area on the north bank of the Arno. This was the workers' district, home to dyers, wool-combers and prostitutes, all of whom lived and worked in a clutter of ramshackle wooden houses.

Filippo thrived in this environment, however, quickly mastering the skill of mounting gems and the complex techniques of niello (engraving on silver) and embossing. At this time he also began studying the science of motion, and, in particular, weights, wheels and gears. The immediate fruits of these investigations were a number of clocks, one of which is even said to have included an alarm bell, making it one of the first alarm clocks ever invented. This clever device – of which, unfortunately, no evidence survives – appears to have been the first of his many stunning technical innovations.[1]

Filippo matriculated as a master goldsmith in 1398, at the age of twenty-one, then rose to city-wide prominence three years later during a competition that, for its intense public interest, rivalled the one between Giovanni di Lapo Ghini and Neri di Fioravanti twenty-five years earlier. This was the famous competition for the bronze doors of the Baptistery of San Giovanni.

This competition – which would play a pivotal role in Filippo's career – came about because of an outbreak of plague. The Black Death was a faithful visitor to Florence. It arrived, on average, once every ten years, always in the summer. After the horrors of 1348, there were further outbreaks, less severe, in 1363, 1374, 1383 and 1390. Various remedies were invented to drive it away. Church bells were violently rung, firearms discharged into the air, and the portrait of the Virgin from the church at nearby Impruneta – an image with miraculous powers that was said to have been painted by St Luke – was borne in procession through the streets. Those rich enough escaped into the country. Those who stayed behind burned wormwood, juniper and lavender in their hearths. Ox-horn and lumps of sulphur were also burned, because stenches were considered equally effective in clearing the air. So intense were these fumigations that sparrows would fall dead from the rooftops.

One of the worst outbreaks occurred in the summer of 1400, when as many as 12,000 Florentines died – that is, just over one person in five. The following year, in order to appease the wrathful deity, the Guild of Cloth Merchants decided to sponsor a new set of bronze doors for San Giovanni. The Baptistery, at whose font every child in Florence was baptised, had long been one of the city's most venerated buildings. An octagonal, marble-encrusted, domed structure standing a few yards to the west of the rising hulk of the new cathedral, it was believed, erroneously, to be a Temple of Mars constructed by Julius Caesar to celebrate the Roman victory over the nearby town of Fiesole (when in fact it was built much later, probably in the seventh century AD). Between 1330 and 1336 the sculptor Andrea Pisano, later one of the cathedral's *capomaestri*, had cast bronze doors to ornament it: twenty panels showing scenes from the life of John the Baptist, the patron saint of Florence. But no further work had

3. The Baptistery of San Giovanni.

since been done to beautify the Baptistery, and Pisano's doors had themselves fallen into disrepair.

Filippo was in Pistoia in 1401, having left Florence because of the plague. There he had been working in collaboration with several other artists on an altar in the cathedral – a prestigious commission – but he returned to Florence immediately upon hearing of the competition. Thirty-four judges were selected from among Florence's numerous artists and sculptors, along with various worthy citizens, including the wealthiest man in Florence, the banker Giovanni di Bicci de' Medici. These judges were charged with choosing the winner from among seven goldsmiths and sculptors, all of them Tuscans.

The plague was not the only threat to Florence at this particular time. No sooner had the pestilence abated than a new danger, potentially worse, hove into view, with serious repercussions for, among other things, Santa Maria del Fiore. Work on the new cathedral had been moving on apace.

The great arches over the main pillars that would support the cupola had been started in 1397 and the chapels on three sides of the octagon were in the process of being vaulted. The Piazza dell'Opera, a triangular space to the east of the cathedral, had been laid out and paved, and a new building had been built to house the Opera del Duomo. Early in 1401, however, this activity abruptly ceased when the Duomo's masons were conscripted into service fortifying the walls of Castellina in Chianti, a small town on the road to Siena. Soon afterwards the Signoria, the executive body of the Republic, hastily ordered them to fortify those of two other towns, Malmantile and Lastra a Signa, both on the road to Pisa.

The reason for this sudden flurry of building was a threat from the north: Giangaleazzo Visconti, the Duke of Milan, against whom the Florentines had fought a war ten years earlier. Giangaleazzo was a ginger-bearded tyrant, cruel and ambitious, whose coat of arms was suitably grisly: a coiled viper crushing in its jaws a tiny, struggling man. His autocratic rule differed drastically from the 'democracy' of Florence, which fulfilled Aristotle's criterion for an ideal republic in that it elected its rulers (albeit with a narrow franchise) to short terms in office. In 1385 Giangaleazzo had seized power in Milan by imprisoning and then poisoning his uncle, Bernabò Visconti, who also happened to be his father-in-law. To befit his new status, Giangaleazzo had bribed the Emperor Wenceslas IV to grant him the title of Duke of Milan. He had also begun work on a new cathedral in Milan, an enormous Gothic structure complete with pinnacles and flying buttresses – precisely the sort of architecture to which Neri di Fioravanti and his group had objected.

It was this old enemy, then, whose shadow now fell over Florence. Not content with his power in northern Italy, Giangaleazzo was proposing to unite the entire peninsula under his rule. Pisa, Siena and Perugia had already been subdued, and by 1401 only Florence stood between him and lordship of all northern and central Italy. Florence was politically and geographically isolated, cut off from the seaports of Pisa and Piombino. Under siege from Giangaleazzo, her trade came to a standstill and famine threatened. The Milanese tyrant even prevented Florence from importing supplies of the wire that was used to make instruments for carding wool. As his troops moved on Florence, the historic rights of the Republic looked doomed.

It was against this background of urgency and crisis that the competition for the second set of bronze doors was played out. The rules of the competition were simple. Each of the candidates was given four sheets of bronze, weighing seventy-five pounds in all, and ordered to execute a scene based on an identical subject: Abraham's sacrifice of Isaac as described in Genesis 22:2–13. This story is traditionally said to prefigure the crucifixion of Christ, but to the Guild of Cloth Merchants, with Florence 'miraculously' delivered from the plague and with Giangaleazzo's armies fast approaching, more immediate analogies may have suggested themselves in this tale of sudden salvation from mortal threat.[2] The competitors were given one year to complete their trial panels, which were to be some 17 inches high by 13 inches wide.

A year may seem like a long time to execute such a relatively small work, but casting in bronze was a delicate operation demanding a high degree of skill. The first step in the process was to model the figure roughly in carefully seasoned clay over which, once the clay had dried, a coating of wax was laid. After the wax had been carved into the shape of the desired statue or relief – work of extreme sculptural precision – a new layer was laid over it: a combination of burnt ox-horn, iron filings and cow dung were mixed together with water, worked into a paste and spread over the wax-coated model with a brush of hog sables. Several layers of soft clay were then applied, each of which was allowed to dry before its successor was overspread. The result was a shapeless mass bound together with iron hoops – the lumpy chrysalis from which the bronze statue was to emerge.

This creation was placed in a kiln and baked until the clay hardened and the layer of wax, as it melted, oozed through small vent holes made for that purpose, usually at the base. A hollow was thereby left into which bronze, melted in a furnace, was poured. The final step in the process was to break away the shapeless husk of baked clay and expose the bronze figure, which could then be chiselled, engraved, polished and, if necessary, gilded. So fraught with opportunities for mishap was the whole process that, in later years, Michelangelo would request a Mass to be said whenever he began pouring a bronze statue.

The trial pieces were completed and the judgement commenced in 1402, as Milanese troops displaying Giangaleazzo's gruesome insignia camped outside the gates of Florence. The prestigious commission would almost certainly make the victor's reputation. Of the original seven competitors, only two were considered worthy of the prize. Filippo Brunelleschi found himself pitted against another young, unknown goldsmith. And so began a lifelong professional rivalry.

Lorenzo Ghiberti was not the most auspicious contender for such a major commission as the Baptistery doors. Only twenty-four years old and with no major works to his credit, he was a member of neither the goldsmiths' nor the sculptors' guilds. Worse still, he was of dubious paternity. Officially the son of a dissolute man named Cione Buonaccorso, he was rumoured to be the illegitimate child of a goldsmith, Bartoluccio Ghiberti, who was now his stepfather.[3] He had apprenticed in Bartoluccio's workshop, assisting in the manufacture of earrings, buttons and various other staples of the goldsmith's trade – hardly tasks on the scale of the Baptistery doors. When plague broke out in 1400, Lorenzo had left for the healthier climate of Rimini, on the Adriatic coast, where he had worked not as a goldsmith but as a painter of murals. He returned to Florence a year later, on the urging of Bartoluccio, who assured him that if he won the commission for the Baptistery doors he need never make another earring.

The two finalists in the competition could not have approached their labours more differently. Lorenzo proved the more cunning tactician, canvassing widely for advice from other artists and sculptors, many of whom happened to be on the jury. Summoned into Bartoluccio's workshop in Santa Croce, they were asked for their opinions of the wax model which, no matter how carefully carved, Lorenzo was always willing to melt and reshape according to their criticisms. Advice was even soliticited from perfect strangers, the dyers and wool-combers of Santa Croce, who were beckoned into the shop as they passed on their way to work. He also made good use of Bartoluccio, who polished the finished work for him.

Filippo, on the other hand, worked in isolation. Secrecy and individual effort were to be two hallmarks of his working habits over the next forty years. Later, whether making architectural models or specialised inventions such as hoists and boats, he insisted on his own solitary authorship, never committing his ideas to paper, or, if he did, only in cipher. He worked either alone or with one or two trusted disciples, always fearful that some unworthy soul would bungle his plans or attempt to steal the credit for them – a nightmare that was later to come true.

In the end, the judges as well as the people of Florence were divided between the merits of the two bronze reliefs – a division that persists among art historians to this day. Filippo's panel is the more dramatic of the two, portraying both Abraham and the angel in histrionic and even violent poses above the contorting figure of Isaac. Lorenzo's figures, on the other hand, appear more graceful and elegant, and his panel was also technically more accomplished inasmuch as it used less bronze and was cast in a single piece. Visitors to Florence can make up their own minds about their respective virtues because the two panels are now preserved in the Museo Nazionale del Bargello. What became of the unsuccessful five is not known. They may well have been melted down during one of Florence's numerous wars – always a danger with bronze. The sixteenth-century Florentine antiquarian and collector Francisco Albertini recommended that goldsmiths who desired immortality should never cast their bronzes in a thickness greater than a knife's edge, because that way they would not be melted down for the casting of cannons. It was all too easy to turn bronze into gun-metal; one had only to add more tin – double the amount used to make bronze – to the alloy. Many of Lorenzo's later pieces appear to have met this fate.

Two conflicting accounts exist of how the thirty-four judges arrived at their final decision. One is courtesy of Lorenzo himself in his autobiography, the *Commentarii*; the other comes from Filippo's first biographer, Antonio di Tuccio Manetti, who, though not born until 1423, claims to have known his subject personally. Neither author is especially disinterested. Lorenzo asserts, with no trace of modesty, that he won the victor's palm 'without a single dissenting voice', whereas in his *Life of Brunelleschi*, written in the 1480s, Manetti relates a more complicated tale in which the judges, unable to decide between the two pieces, reached a compromise and awarded the commission jointly to both men, who were henceforth to work in collaboration. This is not implausible given the size of the project and the relative inexperience of the two young goldsmiths. But Filippo, in Manetti's account, refused to work with Lorenzo, demanding that he alone be given charge of the work. This too sounds plausible considering that Filippo's arrogant self-confidence, irascibility and stubborn unwillingness to work with others is a theme that repeats itself throughout his life.

According to Manetti, Filippo withdrew from the competition when his demand for complete control was refused, leaving the project in the hands of his rival. From that moment, he renounced sculpture – he would never again work in bronze – and quit Florence for Rome. Here he lived intermittently for the next fifteen years, making clocks and setting gems to support himself while he studied the crumbling ruins of ancient Rome. Lorenzo meanwhile was to spend the next twenty-two years at work on the bronze doors, which ultimately weighed ten tons and are acknowledged to be among the great masterpieces of Florentine art.

And what of Giangaleazzo Visconti? As the Milanese armies besieged Florence in the summer of 1402, a holy hermit in the Tuscan countryside prophesied that the tyrant would die before the year was out. As it transpired, the prophecy was fulfilled with several months to spare. In the middle of August, in the sweltering Tuscan heat, just when Florence seemed within his grasp, Giangaleazzo fell ill with a fever, lingered for several weeks, then expired at the beginning of September aged fifty-two. Shortly thereafter the siege was lifted. The Milanese troops disbanded and the blockade was at an end. Florence had been spared and the greatest century in the history of the Republic – what Voltaire calls one of the greatest eras in the history of the world – was ready to commence.

The Treasure Hunters

A CAPITOLIUM, A FORUM, a Temple of Mars, an amphitheatre, an aqueduct, an equestrian statue of Mars on the Ponte Vecchio, Roman baths, assorted walls and towers, to say nothing of the catacombs (*burelle*) which now served as a prison and, less officially, as hide-outs for prostitutes – the citizens of Florence saw ancient Roman ruins wherever they looked in their city.

Or so they believed. The fact is that Florence was not especially rich in Roman remains. Many so-called Roman structures – the Baptistery, for example – actually dated from a much later and more modest era. Nevertheless these observations, however misguided, enjoyed a long and distinguished pedigree, for the historians of Florence were forever inventing spurious links between their city and ancient Rome. The *Chronica de origine civitatis*, an early history written in about 1200, claimed that the city was founded by Julius Caesar. A century later, in his *Convivio*, no less an authority than Dante called Florence 'that beautiful and famous daughter of Rome'. The humanist philosopher Leonardo Bruni agreed with this proud lineage but identified the founder not as Julius Caesar – an imperialist tyrant uncomfortably reminiscent of Giangaleazzo Visconti – but rather as Lucius Cornelius Sulla, who established the city some twenty years before Caesar's reign, during the height of the Roman Republic.

This conviction was given support in 1403 when relics and documents supposedly proving the case were discovered in the church of SS. Apostoli.

Thus when Filippo set off for Rome some time after the end of the competition for the Baptistery doors, patriotic arguments about the Roman origins of the Florentine republic – arguments all the more strident during the years of the Visconti threat[1] – would have been ringing in his ears. Yet in the early 1400s the Eternal City must have been, in most respects, a wretchedly uninspiring sight, a parent that the Florentines may well have wished to disown. A million people had dwelt in Rome during the height of the Empire, but now the city's population was less than that of Florence. The Black Death of 1348 had reduced numbers to 20,000, from which, over the next fifty years, they rose only slightly. Rome had shrunk into a tiny area inside its ancient walls, retreating from the seven hills to huddle among a few streets on the bank of the Tiber across from St Peter's, whose walls were in danger of collapse. Foxes and beggars roamed the filthy streets. Livestock grazed in the Forum, now known as *il Campo Vaccino*, or 'the Field of Cows'. Other monuments had suffered even worse fates. The Temple of Jupiter was a dunghill and both the Theatre of Pompey and the Mausoleum of Augustus had become quarries from which the ancient masonry was scavenged, some of it for buildings as far away as Westminster Abbey. Many ancient statues lay in shards, half-buried, while others had been burned in kilns to make quicklime or else fertiliser for the feeble crops. Still others were mangers for asses and oxen. The funerary monument of Agrippina the Elder, the mother of Caligula, had been turned into a measure for grain and salt.

Rome was a dangerous and unappealing place. There were earthquakes, fevers and endless wars, the latest of which, the War of the Eight Saints, witnessed English mercenaries laying waste to the city. There was no trade or industry apart from the pilgrims who arrived from all over Europe, clutching copies of *Mirabilia urbis romae* ('The Wonders of Rome'), which told them which relics to see during their stay. This guidebook directed them to such holy sights as the finger bone of St Thomas in Santa Croce in Gerusalemme, the arm of St Anne and the head of the Samaritan woman converted by Christ in San Paolo fuori le Mura, or the crib of the infant Saviour in Santa Maria Maggiore. There was a hucksterish atmosphere to the city: pardoners sold indulgences from stalls in the street, and churches advertised confessions that were supposedly good for a remission of infernal torture for a grand total of 8,000 years.

The *Mirabilia urbis romae* did not direct the attention of the pilgrims to the Roman remains that surrounded them. To such pious Christians these ancient ruins were so much heathen idolatry. Worse, they were stained with the blood of Christian martyrs. The Baths of Diocletian, for example, were built with the forced labour of early Christians, many of whom had died during the construction. Antique images that had survived a millennium of earthquakes, erosion and neglect were therefore deliberately trampled underfoot, spat on, or thrown to the ground and smashed to pieces.

Nevertheless, some of the old pagan glory of Rome persisted despite this new breed of Vandal. The high road from the south, the Via Appia, expertly paved with basalt blocks fitted together without mortar, was an architectural marvel in itself, cutting straight as an arrow through mountains, marshes and valleys. Of still more interest were the 300,000 sepulchres that still lined the road for miles, the products of an ancient law that had prevented anyone except the Vestal Virgins and the Emperors from being buried within the walls of Rome. Or one could see the broken arches of aqueducts such as the Acqua Claudia. At 43 miles long, and with arches 100 feet in height, this structure was a testament not only to the fresh drinking water enjoyed by the ancient Romans (in comparison with their descendants, who took their water from the tainted, foul-smelling Tiber) but also to their remarkable engineering skills. Some modern-day Romans were even ignorant of its purpose, believing it to have been used to import olive oil from Naples.

Filippo arrived in this squalid, crumbling city with the talented young Florentine sculptor Donatello, then an adolescent. It was an association that, despite some periods of turbulence, would endure for many years. The pair were well-matched given that Donatello was, if anything, even more hot-tempered than Filippo. A year or two earlier, at the age of fifteen, he had landed himself in trouble with magistrates in Pistoia for striking a German over the head with a large stick, and many years later he would travel to Ferrara intent upon murdering one of his runaway apprentices. His patrons likewise felt his wrath: if one of them refused to pay the full price for a statue, Donatello would demolish it in a fit of temper.

The two young men lived like vagabonds, paying little attention to what they ate, how they dressed, or where they slept. Together they began digging among the vast ruins, hiring porters to cart away the rubble and becoming known to locals as the 'treasure hunters' because it was believed they were searching for gold coins and other treasures – an impression reinforced whenever they excavated earthenware pots filled with antique medals. Their activities may have attracted suspicion and even fear, not merely because they were suspected of practising geomancy (the art of divining the future by interpreting the patterns made by handfuls of scattered earth), but because pagan fragments were considered bad luck. In the fourteenth century, for example, the Sienese had unearthed an ancient Roman statue and, after placing it on the fountain in their main piazza, suffered a military defeat at the hands of the Florentines. The statue was promptly removed from the piazza and, in order to curse their enemies, reburied in Florentine territory.

What exactly Filippo sought in these excavations was unknown even to Donatello. Antonio Manetti claims that Filippo, secretive as ever, made his study of the ancient ruins while pretending to be doing something else. He inscribed on strips of parchment a series of cryptic symbols and Arabic numbers: a secret code, that is, like the reversed handwriting that Leonardo da Vinci would later use to describe his own inventions. Before patents or copyrights, scientists frequently resorted to ciphers in order to conceal their discoveries from jealous rivals. Two centuries earlier the Oxford philosopher Roger Bacon, known as 'Doctor Mirabilis' for his experiments with telescopes, flying machines and robots, claimed that no scientist should ever write of his discoveries in plain language but must resort instead to 'concealed writing'.*

What was the purpose of Filippo's cryptic symbols and Arabic numerals, the latter of which the Commune of Florence had banned in 1296?[2] Manetti claims he was surveying the antiquities of Rome, measuring their heights and proportions. He fails to record what method Filippo used, but he could have determined the height of columns or buildings with an upright rod. This method would have been familiar to him from Leonardo Fibonacci's *Practica geometriae*, a work that was studied in the schools of Florence. Or he could have employed a quadrant or, even more simply, a mirror, whose use for mensuration Fibonacci likewise describes. The surveyor placed the mirror on the ground some distance in front of the object to be measured, then moved himself into a position such that the top of the object appeared in the centre of the mirror. The height of the building was then calculated by multiplying the distance between the object and the mirror by the height of the observer divided by his own distance from the glass.

Filippo was not the first person to survey the ruins of Rome. As early as 1375 Giovanni de' Dondi, the famous clockmaker, measured the obelisk of St Peter's, a process which he described in his book *Roman Journey*. But the knowledge that Filippo sought to uncover was unique. In calculating the proportions of columns and pediments he determined the measurements specific to the three architectural orders (Doric, Ionic and Corinthian) that had been invented by the Greeks and then imitated and refined by the

---

* The history of science is full of such codes. The English scientist and inventor Robert Hooke would keep secret his discovery of the law of elasticity by means of an anagram – CEIIINOSSSTUU – which, once unscrambled, read UT TENSIO SIC VIS ('As the elongation, so the force'). There were, naturally, pitfalls to this method of encryptment. Galileo used a cipher to announce to Johann Kepler his discovery of the rings of Saturn, an anagram which, once unscrambled, should have read: OBSERVO ALTISSIMUM PLANETAM TERGEMINIM ('I have observed the most distant of planets to have a triple form'). Kepler, however, translated it thus: SALUE UMBISTINEUM GEMINATUM MARTIA PROLES ('Hail, twin companionship, children of Mars'), thereby leading to the longstanding erroneous notion that Saturn was possessed of two moons.

Romans. These orders were governed by precise mathematical ratios, a series of proportional rules that regulated aesthetic effect. The height of a Corinthian entablature, for example, is a quarter of the height of the columns on which it stands, while the height of each column is ten times its diameter, and so forth. Numerous examples of these three orders existed in Rome in the early 1400s. The columns in the Baths of Diocletian are Doric, for instance, while those at the Temple of Fortuna Virilis feature the Ionic, and the portico of the Pantheon the Corinthian. The Colosseum makes use of all three: Doric on the lowest level, Ionic on the second, and Corinthian at the top.[3]

Knowing that a dome was planned for the cathedral in Florence – a dome that no one as yet knew how to build – Filippo must have taken a special interest in the methods of vaulting used by the ancient Romans. In the early years of the fifteenth century any number of domes would have been available for him to scrutinise. After large parts of the city were burned in the fire of AD 64, Nero had established regulations (much like those adopted after the Great Fire of London in 1666) that widened the streets, controlled the water supply and – most vital from an architectural perspective – restricted the use of inflammable building materials. The Romans therefore started to use concrete, a new invention, in their buildings. The secret of Roman concrete was in its mortar which contained a volcanic ash made available by active volcanoes such as Vesuvius. Combined with lime mortar, it resulted in a strong, fast-setting cement to which an aggregate of small broken stones was added. Unlike conventional mortars made from quicklime, sand and water, which set only when the water evaporates, 'pozzolana concrete' (as it is known) combines chemically with water so that, like modern Portland cement, it cures swiftly, even under water. Although various Roman baths had been vaulted in concrete since the first century BC, extensive and inventive use of concrete arches and domes was made only after the fire of AD 64. The history of domes commences, effectively, with the opportunities created by this great conflagration – one that the Romans believed was either the work of Nero himself or else that of the wrathful gods.

The Domus Aurea, or the Golden House of Nero, begun immediately after the fire by the architects Severus and Celer, shows the confident use of concrete to exploit new architectural shapes. This splendid urban palace stretched from the Palatine to the Esquiline across an area that had been decimated by the fire. Enormously expensive to build, it contained elaborate decorations, including the *Laocoön* (which would be rediscovered there in 1506), and mechanical wonders such as pipes concealed in the ceiling of the dining hall that sprayed perfumes on the Emperor's dinner guests. Its most interesting architectural feature, however, is an octagonal room in the east wing that is roofed by a dome whose span is some 35 feet across. The octagonal shape must have interested Filippo, who would have known, of course, that the dome of Santa Maria del Fiore, though much larger, was also intended to be eight-sided.

Of even more interest to Filippo would have been the Pantheon, the Emperor Hadrian's temple to the gods of all the planets, executed between AD 118 and 128. Unlike the octagonal cupola in the Domus Aurea, the dome of the Pantheon is colossal, spanning 142 feet internally and rising to a height of 143 feet. Almost thirteen centuries after its construction it was still the largest dome ever built and it had escaped plunder because it was now converted into a church, Santa Maria Rotonda. The modern Romans and pilgrims alike were amazed by the immense dome. With no visible signs of support, it seemed to defy the laws of nature. They called it the 'house of devils', attributing its construction not to the skilled engineers of the ancient world but rather to the sinister forces of demons.

What structural features of this 'house of devils' might Filippo have studied? The architects of the Pantheon faced the statical problems encountered by builders of all domes: how to counteract the forces that act on any vault. These forces are separated into 'push' and 'pull' energies, known respectively as compression and tension. All elements in a building – its columns, arches, walls, roof beams – are subject to one or other of these actions: their stone or timber beams are compressed from above (which causes them to shorten) or pulled from the side (which causes them to stretch). An architect must design a structure

4. The Pantheon.

that will counteract these pressures by playing them off against each other – a game of action and reaction – and channelling them safely to the ground.

The first type of pressure does not create insurmountable problems for an architect. Stone, brick and concrete all possess such enormous compressive strengths that buildings can be raised to colossal heights without the blocks of stone crushing at the base. The tallest spire in England, that of Salisbury Cathedral, stands 404 feet high, and the two towers of the cathedral in Cologne each rise to 511 feet, or the equivalent of a fifty-storey building. At this height they are almost a dozen feet taller than the Great Pyramid at Giza, another edifice whose tremendous size is made possible by the strength of the stone blocks from which it was built. Yet not even these soaring structures come close to exhausting the compressive strength of stone: a column of limestone could be built to a height of 12,000 feet, or over two miles high, before starting to crush under its own weight.

The stones in a dome, however, are not only crushed from above but also thrust outward by the pull energy known as 'hoop stress', in the same way as the rubber of an inflated balloon will bulge outwards if one compresses it from above. The problem for architects is that stone and brick do not respond nearly so well to this lateral thrust as to compression.

The Romans seem to have possessed some understanding of the structural problems created by tension and compression and they attempted to solve them by making extensive use of the new pozzolana concrete. Where the horizontal stress is greatest, at the base of the dome, the concrete wall of the Pantheon was built to a massive thickness of 23 feet. It then tapers to only two feet at the top, at which point a round window or 'oculus' is left open. Five thousand tons of concrete were poured in horizontal layers on to wooden formwork, but at the top of the dome lightweight aggregates such as pumice and, more inventive still, empty *amphorae* (clay bottles used for shipping olive oil) were added to the concrete in place of stone in order to reduce the load. The inside of the

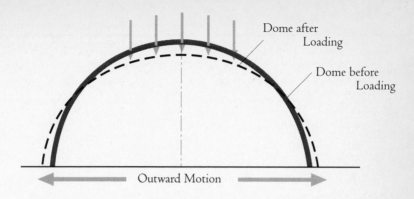

5. Hoop stress. The dotted line shows how the dome is deformed by weight at the top.

dome was also coffered, which not only lightened the load still further but also added a decorative feature that has since been extensively imitated.

The Pantheon would have presented Filippo with proof that it was possible to span a space as vast as that at Santa Maria del Fiore. Yet Hadrian's architects were not entirely successful, for a series of cracks are visible along the inside of the dome, running like lightning strokes down the ceiling to the springing line, the point where the dome begins to curve inwards. These fractures are the result of the hoop stress that causes the dome to spread at its haunches, stretching the fabric horizontally around the circumference. Filippo could have seen a similar pattern of radial cracks around the base of the semidome in the Baths of Trajan, and indeed such cracks have been an all too common feature of masonry domes. Containment of this horizontal stress – one that it appears not even a concrete wall 23 feet thick could neutralise – was therefore of paramount importance in constructing a stable cupola. For all their ingenuity, not even the Romans, it seemed, could provide the solution to the challenge laid down by Neri di Fioravanti and his committee.

It is not known exactly how long Filippo stayed in Rome or when precisely he left. He appears to have lived there, off and on, for more than ten years, with occasional returns to Florence. His stay in Rome was one of the first examples of a new kind of quest. Pilgrims of a different variety soon began arriving in the city, ones seeking relics other than the bones of saints on display in the Christian churches. The image of Rome would be transformed during the Renaissance. Far from being condemned for its pagan associations, the ancient city came to be venerated for its architecture, its statuary and its learning. The architects Leon Battista Alberti, Antonio Filarete, Francesco di Giorgio and Michelangelo were all to follow in Filippo's footsteps, travelling to Rome to take their inspiration from the ruins. No longer was it considered bad luck to unearth pagan remains, either in Rome (where Cicero's house was excavated) or elsewhere. In 1413, for example, the bones of the Roman historian Livy were exhumed in Padua, causing an outburst of almost religious fervour. The bones were enshrined in Padua's Town Hall, and soon afterwards the city fathers received from Alfonso, King of Naples, the urgent request for a femur. An even more spectacular relic was the perfectly preserved body of a young Roman girl excavated from one of the tombs along the Via Appia and exhibited to the populace of Rome in 1485.

Other treasures were also discovered. Manuscripts were disinterred from where they had lain entombed throughout the centuries. The *Annals* of Tacitus, Cicero's *Orator* and *De oratore*, the poems of Tibullus, Propertius and Catullus (the lone manuscript of whose work was found stoppering a wine barrel), the *Satyricon* of Petronius, the poems of Lucretius, a complete copy of Quintilian's *Institutio oratoria* – all of these shards of ancient Rome, lost or unknown for centuries, were recovered in the first decades of the fifteenth century. Like the fragments of stone studied by Filippo, such manuscripts would form a link between the ancient Romans and the artists, philosophers and architects of the Quattrocento. And it was from these broken stones and faded parchments that the world would now be made afresh.

An Ass and a Babbler

WHEN HE RETURNED permanently to Florence, probably in 1416 or 1417, Filippo moved back into his childhood home near the cathedral, a good vantage point for a man obsessed with the architectural puzzle presented by the dome to survey its progress. He would have found that much had been accomplished on the cathedral. The tambour, or drum, had been constructed between 1410 and 1413, with walls fourteen feet thick in order to support the weight of the cupola. In 1413 a large new crane had been built to raise materials, and two of the three tribunes of the octagon had been vaulted. The church had also just acquired its new name, Santa Maria del Fiore, 'Our Lady of the Flowers', having previously been referred to as Santa Reparata, the name of the older cathedral which was now completely demolished.

Now in middle age, Filippo was short, bald and pugnacious-looking, with an aquiline nose, thin lips and a weak chin. His appearance was not helped by his dirty and dishevelled clothing. Yet in Florence such an unsightly display was almost a badge of genius, and Filippo was simply the latest in a long and illustrious line of ugly or unkempt artists. The name of the painter Cimabue means 'ox-head', and Giotto was so unattractive that Giovanni Boccaccio devoted a tale to his appearance in the *Decameron*, marvelling at how 'Nature has frequently planted astonishing genius in men of monstrously ugly appearance'. Later, Michelangelo would become legendary for his ugliness, which was partly the result of a broken nose earned in a fracas with the sculptor Pietro Torrigiani. And like both Giotto and Filippo, Michelangelo was indifferent to the state of his dress, often going for months on end without changing his dogskin breeches. In the end, ugly and eccentric artists would become so much the norm that Filippo's biographer, the painter and architect Giorgio Vasari – himself an uncouth man, with a skin disease and dirty, uncut fingernails – marvelled that an artist as talented as Raphael should actually have been physically handsome.

Perhaps unsurprisingly, Filippo was unmarried. But although in Florence bachelorhood was not unusual for a man in his forties, since men married late and generally took much younger women as their brides, Filippo would never marry, and in this abstention from family life he also became part of a long and glorious tradition of artists that included Donatello, Masaccio, Leonardo da Vinci and Michelangelo. Many Florentine artists and thinkers took a dim view of both marriage and women. Boccaccio, who never married, had criticised Dante for having done so, claiming that a wife was a hindrance to study.

No sooner was he settled in Florence than Filippo took steps to become involved in the cupola project. In May 1417 the Opera del Duomo paid him 10 florins for drawing plans of the dome on parchment. What these plans showed is not recorded, but Manetti reports that Filippo's advice had been eagerly sought by the wardens after his return from Rome. That he should have insinuated his way into the heart of such an important project at this stage is possibly surprising, regardless of his growing reputation as a student of Roman vaulting techniques. Despite his youthful promise as a metalworker he had, at the age of forty-one, accomplished relatively little in practical terms. In 1412 he had given advice on the construction of the cathedral in the nearby town of Prato, but the work being done there was decorative rather than structural, entailing the encrustation of the church's façade with the dark-green stone known as serpentine. And so far he had failed to receive a single architectural commission except for a house near the Mercato Vecchio that he had built for his kinsman Apollonio Lapi.

By 1418 Filippo was probably best known for an experiment in linear perspective. This experiment must have been conducted in or before 1413, when Domenico da Prato refers to him as 'the perspective expert, ingenious man, Filippo di Ser Brunellesco, remarkable for skill and fame'. It was one of the first of Filippo's many innovations and a landmark in the history of painting.

Perspective is the method of representing three-dimensional objects in recession on a two-dimensional surface in order to give the same impression of relative position, size or distance as the actual objects do when viewed from a particular point. Filippo is generally regarded as its inventor, the one who discovered (or rediscovered) its mathematical laws. For example, he worked out the principle of the vanishing point, which was known to the Greeks and Romans but, like so much other knowledge, had long since been lost. Greek vase paintings and marble reliefs show an understanding of perspective, as do some of the scene paintings for Greek tragedies staged in Athens, including those of Aeschylus. The Roman scientist Pliny the Elder claimed that this method of representation (which he calls *imagines obliquae*, or 'slanting images') had been invented by a painter of the sixth century BC named Kimon of Kleonai. The Romans made use of perspective in their wall paintings, and some of its principles were described by the architect Vitruvius. Furthermore, it seems inconceivable that buildings such as the Pantheon or the Colosseum could have been built without their architects executing perspective drawings of some sort.

After the decline of the Roman Empire, however, the technique of perspective drawing was lost or abandoned. Plato had condemned perspective as a deceit, and the Neoplatonist philosopher Plotinus (AD 205–270) praised the flattened art of the ancient Egyptians for showing figures in their 'true' proportions. This prejudice against the 'dishonesty' of perspective was adopted in Christian art, with the result that naturalistic space was renounced throughout the Middle Ages. Only in the first decades of the fourteenth century did the ancient methods of perspective reappear when Giotto began using chiaroscuro – a treatment of light and shade – to create realistic three-dimensional effects.

Filippo might have seen examples of ancient perspective painting during his travels through Italy. But he probably worked out the principles of perspective from quite different sources. The procedures for executing his own painting – plotting lines of sight on a plane surface – he could have learned from the surveying techniques he employed while measuring the ruins of Rome.[1] Perspective drawing is, after all, similar to surveying in that both involve determining the relative positions of three-dimensional objects for the purpose of protracting them on paper or canvas. The practice of measuring and surveying was highly developed by Filippo's time: his great leap appears to have been an application of its principles and techniques to the art of painting.

Filippo's experiment consisted of an almost magical optical trick, a *trompe l'oeil* painting that, in its clever confusion of life and art, prefigured much later experiments with optical devices such as camera obscuras, panoramas, dioramas and catoptric art. This painting – one of the most famous in the history of art – has long since been lost to the world. Last known to have been in the possession of Lorenzo the Magnificent, it vanished after the occupation of Florence by Charles VIII of France in 1494, when many works of Florentine art were looted. It was clearly described, however, by Antonio Manetti, who claimed to have held it in his hands and attempted the experiment himself.

For the subject of his perspective painting Filippo chose one of Florence's most familiar sights: the Baptistery of San Giovanni. Positioning himself a short distance inside the middle portal of Santa Maria del Fiore, some 115 feet from the Baptistery, he painted on to a small panel, in perfect perspective, using a geometrically constructed picture plane, everything that was visible through the 'frame' of the cathedral's doorway: the Baptistery and its surrounding streets, including the wafer-makers in the Casa della Misericordia and the corner of the sheep market. In place of a painted sky he substituted a piece of burnished silver, a mirror that would reflect the clouds, birds and changing sunlight of the actual sky. Finally, he drilled a small hole the size of a lentil bean into the vanishing point of the painting, or that central point on the horizon where the receding parallel lines appear to converge.

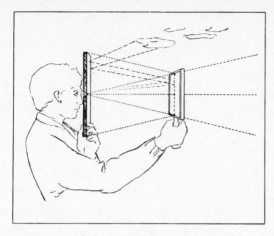

6. Diagram of the optical instrument used by Brunelleschi to render the Baptistery in perspective. The painting is on the left, the mirror on the right.

The panel was then ready for demonstration. Standing six feet inside the doorway of Santa Maria del Fiore – on the exact spot, in other words, where Filippo had executed the panel – the observer was to turn the painted side of the panel away from himself and peer through the small aperture. In his other hand he was to hold a mirror, the reflection of which, when the glass was held at arm's length, showed (in reverse) the painted image of the Baptistery and the Piazza San Giovanni. So lifelike was this reflection that the observer was unable to tell whether the peephole revealed the actual scene that should have been before him – the 'real scene' lying beyond the panel – or only a perfect illusion of that reality.

When the competition for the model of the dome was announced in August 1418, Filippo must have jumped at the chance. In June the aged and infirm *capomaestro* Giovanni d'Ambrogio, who had been called back into service from retirement in 1415 following the premature death of his successor, Antonio di Banco, had built a model for the cupola's scaffolding. But this model cannot have been especially inspiring as the Opera saw fit to invite other attempts only two months later. With the prize of 200 florins at stake, Filippo and eleven other competitors hopefully submitted their models. The 1367 model was still sacrosanct, of course: the problem at hand was its practical execution.

How to build the invisible supports demanded by the model – the circumferential chains that had been the subject of such debate in 1366–7 – was still a vexed question. Also essential to the project was the resolution of a difficulty not fully considered by Neri and his group: the temporary wooden framework, or 'centring', needed to support the masonry of the dome while the mortar cured. Except in the Near East, where there was a shortage of strong timber, all masonry vaults were (and still are) constructed on wooden frameworks that are supported either by scaffolding or from the ground. In the cases of most small-span arches the process is relatively simple. A timber centre is built to the desired profile in order to support the stones comprising the arch. This structure has to be both strong enough to bear the weight of the masonry and rigid enough to resist bending under the incremental loading of the blocks of stone. It also has to be easy to remove when the time comes.

7. Wooden centring supporting an arch.

It is sometimes possible to build perfectly spherical domes without this sort of centring because each circular layer of masonry forms a self-sustaining horizontal arch. As one of Filippo's friends, Leon Battista Alberti, explained in his treatise on architecture: 'The spherical vault, unique among vaults, does not require centring because it is composed not only of arches but of superimposed rings.' Each stone or brick, that is, forms part of a horizontal as well as a vertical arch and is therefore held in place by the pressures of the surrounding masonry. But the shape of the cupola in Florence, dictated by the 1367 model, was not circular but octagonal and pointed, meaning that the horizontal courses of masonry would not be continuous, as in a circular dome, but broken at each of the eight corners.

The construction of a wooden centring for the dome of Santa Maria del Fiore therefore appeared essential. Yet its design presented the wardens with major difficulties, both technical and financial, first and foremost because the centring, like the dome itself, would have to be a structure unprecedented in scale. Innumerable trees had to be found for the required timber. As the competition was being proclaimed, thirty-two large tree trunks were delivered to the Opera and cut into 900 feet of planks and 135 stripped beams for use in the scaffolding, centring and loading platform of the south tribune of the cathedral, now ready for vaulting. The cupola, however, was to be much larger than the tribune and would therefore have required, in one estimate, twenty times as much wood, or as many as 700 trees.[2] The Opera owned a number of forests on the slopes of the Apennines, but timber was rivalled only by marble for its expense and the logistical difficulties of its acquisition, being in short supply and, in the absence of hydraulic saws, extremely labour intensive. It was perhaps an omen that the *capomaestro* Antonio di Banco died while on a trip in search of timber supplies with which to build the centring for the dome.

Even if sufficient numbers of good quality trees could be found, and even if the expense of sawing the wood and assembling the vast structure could be absorbed, other problems would have confronted the wardens. The act of decentring — the removal of the wood from beneath the finished vault — was one of the most hazardous operations in the entire building process. During the Middle Ages the most usual method of decentring was to set the supporting poles of the centre's scaffolding in sand-filled kegs and then, at the time of striking, to unplug the kegs and allow the sand to escape, thereby slowly lowering the level of the wooden framework. This operation may seem simple, but timing was a major problem. Medieval mortars remained 'green' for up to a year or even eighteen months, until the water necessary for crystallisation had completely evaporated. The centring for the vaults of the south tribune, for example, remained in place for thirteen months, from June 1420 until

July 1421, thus tying up a large amount of timber that could have been reused elsewhere – for example, in the loading platform for the cupola. If centring was struck too early, the mortar would still be plastic and its strength insufficient. On the other hand, long-term loadings create a deformation of wood known to engineers as 'creep': if the centring was left in place for too long the timber would warp beneath the weight of the vault it supported, causing the masonry to shift. This phenomenon was known to the ancient Greeks, who would remove the wheels of their chariots at night, or else prop the chariots vertically against a wall (as Telemachus does in Book IV of the *Odyssey*) in order to prevent the wheels from warping under the weight of the stationary vehicles.

A final difficulty was that the centring for such a massive dome would have been awkward and obtrusive, even when erected in an area as large as the cathedral's central octagon. Vast in scale, running from the ground to the oculus – the open window at the top of the dome – it would have crowded the octagon and left little room for the masons to manoeuvre.

One design for the dome's centring existed already, a legacy of Giovanni di Lapo Ghini, the *capomaestro* whose plan for the cupola had lost out to Neri di Fioravanti's. His wooden model of the centring, executed in 1371, sat inside Neri's 1367 model. But evidently this model, like that of Giovanni d'Ambrogio, was inadequate to the task.

By the end of August, barely two weeks into the competition, Filippo had already begun building a brick model of the cupola. The wardens of the Opera appointed four master masons to assist with its construction. They must have been taken aback by what they saw, perhaps suspecting Filippo of preparing a clever illusion like his painting of the Baptistery, one that would deceive the senses and defy the laws of reason. As with his panel, Filippo set about his task with meticulous craftsmanship. For the woodwork he had hired two of Florence's most gifted sculptors, his friend Donatello and also Nanni di Banco, the son of the late *capomaestro* and a man who had worked on the cathedral for over ten years. The four masons sent from the Opera spent a total of ninety days working on the model.

Constructed in one of the courtyards of the Opera, Filippo's model was the size of a small building, requiring forty-nine cartloads of quicklime and over 5,000 bricks. It had a span of over six feet and stood twelve feet tall, easily high enough for the wardens and various consultants to walk inside to inspect it. And like many architectural models it must also have been an exquisitely rendered work of art, for the carvings by Donatello and Nanni di Banco – two men whose brilliantly lifelike sculptures adorned the façade and side portals of the cathedral – had been gilded and painted by the artist Stefano del Nero.

Although the competition was originally intended to end on 30 September, it was extended by two more months, perhaps to allow Filippo to complete his elaborate model, or to give some of his rivals, masters from Pisa and Siena, time to transport themselves and their models to Florence. Not until December 1418 did a Great Council consisting of the thirteen wardens along with consuls of the Wool Guild and various consultants assemble in the nave of the cathedral to consider the various designs. After bread and wine were served, the models were discussed. Filippo's brick model in particular received a good deal of attention, both on 7 December and then a fortnight later, when its merits were debated over a period of four days.

The documents of the Opera del Duomo record these bare facts and nothing more. But Filippo's two biographers, Manetti and Vasari, relate a livelier tale. Despite assurances in the original proclamation of August 1418 that all models would find a *bene et gratiose audietur* – a 'friendly and trustworthy audience' – Filippo's proposal was greeted by the wardens and its chosen experts with scepticism and even, at times, outright hostility.

The reasons for these reactions are not difficult to understand. Filippo had approached the problem of the centring in a revolutionary manner, one utterly different from his rivals'. Everyone else took it for granted that an elaborate framework would be required to support the masonry of the rising dome; the only questions were ones of economics and design. One of the proposals put forward involved sustaining the cupola on a temporary mound of earth piled to a height of 300 feet. This project is not actually as ridiculous as it might sound since Romanesque vaults were sometimes built over rooms that had been filled with earth. Indeed, as late as 1496, soil heaped to a height of 98 feet was used as a centring for the vaults in the cathedral at Troyes. But the proposal was met with derision in the Great Council. One of the wardens suggested, with withering sarcasm, that coins should be mixed into the dirt so that when the time came to decentre the immense vault the citizens of Florence would be eager to lend a helping hand.

Filippo, on the other hand, offered a simpler and more daring solution: he proposed to do away with the centring altogether. This was an astounding proposal. Even the smallest arches were built over wooden centring. How then would it be possible to span the enormous diameter called for in the 1367 model without any support, particularly when the bricks at the top of the vault would be inclined at 60-degree angles to the horizontal? So astonishing was the plan that many of Filippo's contemporaries considered him a lunatic. And it has likewise confounded more recent commentators who are reluctant to believe that such a feat could actually have been possible.[3]

Filippo did himself few favours when he appeared before the Great Council to expound his revolutionary design. Anxious, as usual, that no one should steal the fruits of his ingenuity, he stubbornly refused to divulge to the wardens the explicit technical details of his plans. The wardens, naturally, were little impressed by this sort of coyness. They pressed Filippo to elaborate. He refused. So heated did the exchanges become, according to Vasari, that he was first derided as 'an ass and a babbler', then physically ejected from one of the more unpleasant assemblies. Many years later he would confide to Antonio Manetti that he had been ashamed to show his face in the street for fear of being taunted as 'that madman who utters such nonsense'. His ingenious plan looked like a lost cause.

Filippo was naturally incensed by this treatment, and the experience served to confirm his low opinion of what, ten years later, he would call 'the ignorant crowd'. But in Florence, as Vasari notes, no one's opinion remains unchanged for long. Just what won the wardens round to the merits of Filippo's project is unclear. Vasari relates an anecdote that is as amusing as it is improbable – a legend like that of Archimedes in his bathtub or Newton under the apple tree. In this parable Filippo suggests to the wardens that whoever can make an egg stand on end on a flat piece of marble should win the commission. When all of the other contestants fail the test, Filippo simply cracks the egg on the bottom and then stands it upright. When his rivals protest that they might have done the same, Filippo retorts that they would know how to vault the cupola, too, if only they knew his plans. And so the commission, Vasari claims, promptly went to Filippo.

It seems unlikely in the extreme that the serious-minded wool magnates of the Opera del Duomo would be tempted to hand over the commission on the basis of such a parlour trick. Implausible as the story sounds, however, it is worth noting how the humble egg has long fascinated scientists and engineers. Both Alexander of Aphrodisia and Pliny the Elder marvelled at the longitudinal strength of this apparently flimsy structure that, as the latter states, 'no human force can break'. Galileo, too, would ponder the phenomenon. In a fragment dedicated to his son he enquires: 'Why is it that an egg held with your hands by its top and bottom and pressed with great force cannot be crushed?' His pupil Vincenzo Viviani resumed the topic, going so far as to speculate that the egg – or, rather, a half eggshell, placed upside down – was the inspiration behind the architecture of the domed vault.

The egg anecdote aside, the results of the deliberations by the Opera were not as clear-cut and decisive as Vasari implies, though in December 1418 most of the other models were indeed eliminated from consideration. The panel of judges fixed their attention on the two remaining designs, one of which would be selected as the basis for the dome's construction. History had begun repeating itself. The first model was, of course, Filippo's. The second, also made of brick, and also built in one of the Opera's courtyards, had been designed by his old adversary, Lorenzo Ghiberti.

5

The Rivals

THE PREVIOUS SIXTEEN years had treated Filippo's fellow goldsmith very well. At the age of forty, Lorenzo Ghiberti had become one of the most renowned artists in all of Italy. He was bald like Filippo but, unlike Filippo, looked merry and avuncular, with a moon face and a large, fleshy nose. As was the custom in Florence, he had married late, at the age of thirty-seven, taking as his bride a sixteen-year-old, Marsilia, the daughter of a wool-comber, who promptly gave him two sons. Most of his time was spent in his workshop opposite the convent of Santa Maria Novella, where, after almost two decades of work, he was still busy casting the doors for the Baptistery in a giant, purpose-built furnace. Thus far he had melted almost 6,000 pounds of bronze for the project.

Lorenzo was a prosperous man by now, with a house in Florence and a vineyard in the country. As his stepfather Bartoluccio had prophesied in 1401, he was no longer required to make earrings for a living. Since winning the competition for the Baptistery doors he had been kept busy with commissions: tombs in marble or bronze, candelabras, shrines, reliefs for the baptismal font in Siena Cathedral and a bronze statue of St John the Baptist for the Guild of Cloth Merchants. Completed in 1414 and installed in a niche at Orsanmichele, this statue, at almost nine feet tall, was the largest work in bronze ever cast in Florence – a testament to Lorenzo's ambition and skill.

But Lorenzo, for all of this work, had precious little experience as an architect. Indeed, his model for the cupola marks his first foray into that field. In contrast to Filippo's, his model was neither large nor intricate. His four masons worked only four days each on it compared with the ninety spent on Filippo's. It was made from *mattoni picholini*, or small bricks, and presumably involved some sort of centring, for Lorenzo also employed a carpenter in its construction.[1] This was probably the fundamental difference between the two models which the wardens found themselves obliged to choose between.

The flurry of activity in the last months of 1418 was followed by a lull of more than a year. No firm decisions were made. Christmas arrived: the wardens ordered geese for themselves. On New Year's Day, as usual, they swore their oath to build the dome according to Neri di Fioravanti's model. Then for a number of months they dithered and delayed. The cupola project languished. No one – neither Filippo nor Lorenzo – was awarded the prize of 200 florins.

One of the reasons for the delay was that a crack was discovered in the vaulting of the north tribune. This vault had been raised little more than ten years earlier, so its fracture was hardly an auspicious sign under which to begin raising an enormous and structurally uncertain cupola. Another reason was that old Giovanni d'Ambrogio had been removed from his post as *capomaestro*, having become too decrepit to ascend to the top of the vault to inspect the work of the stonemasons. A third reason was that, one month after the Great Council, events temporarily overcame the cupola project: in January 1419 Pope Martin V and his entourage arrived in Florence.

Martin V had been elected pope several years earlier at the Council of Constance, which ended the Great Schism, the 39-year period in which the Roman Catholic Church was divided between rival popes in Rome and Avignon. The Council had deposed John XXIII, a one-time pirate and dedicated libertine who was said to have seduced hundreds of women, and replaced him with Martin. The new pope would remain in Florence for the next twenty months, until Rome could be properly fortified and some of its churches restored. In the meantime Florence had to be made hospitable for His Holiness. The Opera del Duomo therefore diverted masons and carpenters from the cathedral to Santa Maria Novella, where a sumptuous set of apartments was hastily contrived, complete with a staircase that the Opera commissioned from Lorenzo after a competition involving two other designs. This verdict must have augured well, in Lorenzo's mind, for the Opera's other, much larger commission.

Filippo bided his time fruitfully during these months. He refined his model, adding both a lantern and a circular gallery around the drum. But by now he, like Lorenzo, was involved with other projects. The year 1419 was, for him, an *annus mirabilis* of sorts. In the six months following the cupola competition he received four separate architectural commissions, all in Florence. This is remarkable in light of the fact that he had won no prior commissions. It suggests that, for all the ridicule to which they were subjected, his plans for the dome had won him a good deal of respect.

The first of these commissions was the Ridolfi Chapel in San Jacopo sopr'Arno, south of the river, and the Barbadori Chapel nearby in Santa Felìcita. Then came the sacristy in San Lorenzo, commissioned by the wealthy banker Giovanni de' Medici, who hoped to be entombed inside Filippo's creation. Finally there was the Ospedale degli Innocenti, the 'Hospital of the Innocents', a home for abandoned infants sponsored by the Silk Merchants, the guild responsible for the welfare of the Commune's foundlings and orphans. It was also in 1419 that Filippo adopted, and then apprenticed, a seven-year-old orphan named Andrea Cavalcanti, later known as Il Buggiano, after his home village in Tuscany. This was to be a productive if occasionally turbulent association.

It was no coincidence that three of the four commissions awarded to Filippo in 1419 included cupolas. Particularly significant were the Barbadori Chapel and the Ridolfi Chapel. Both of these were commissioned by members of the Wool Guild, therefore by men closely involved with the cupola project at Santa Maria del Fiore.[2] These two chapels represented tests for Filippo, serving as trial runs for the novel scheme of vaulting without centring. Unfortunately, nothing now remains of either dome. The interior of San Jacopo was rebuilt in 1709, and in 1589 the dome of the Barbadori Chapel was demolished by Vasari (ironically, Filippo's ardent champion) when the long corridor was built to link the Pitti Palace to the Uffizi. It is therefore impossible to know whether the techniques Filippo used were those he later employed on the cupola of Santa Maria del Fiore. What we do know is that both domes were raised without wooden centring, although ironically the one for the Ridolfi Chapel was actually smaller than Filippo's brick model.

Towards the end of 1419 the Wool consuls made a concerted effort to resolve the problem of the dome by appointing four men to a special *ad hoc* committee known as the *Uffitiales Cupule*. These 'Four Officials of the Cupola' moved swiftly. On 16 April 1420 they assembled the thirteen wardens and twenty-four Wool consuls in the headquarters of the guild, the Palazzo dell'Arte della Lana, several streets south of the cathedral, in order to appoint a new *capomaestro* to replace Giovanni d'Ambrogio. Their choice was a thirty-eight-year-old master mason named Battista d'Antonio who had served as *vice-capomaestro* under Giovanni. Battista had worked on the cathedral site since 1398, first as an apprentice stonemason, then as a master. Eight other master masons were then appointed to serve under Battista, each being placed in charge of one of the eight sides of the octagonal dome.

So omnipresent would Battista d'Antonio become at Santa Maria del Fiore over the next thirty years, and so neglected has his role been, that he has been called the 'hunchback of the Duomo'.[3] Despite his title as *capomaestro*, however, he was actually more a foreman or overseer than an architect or designer in the mould of previous *capomaestri* such as Giotto or Andrea Pisano. These two men were first and foremost artists, the one having trained as a painter, the other as a goldsmith. Battista, on the other hand, was a mason and, like most masons, worked in traditional ways and according to long-established rules and precedents, imitating previous designs rather than inventing new ones. He would become the on-site supervisor whose task it was to translate any models and plans settled upon by the Opera del Duomo into bricks-and-mortar reality by co-ordinating the efforts of the eight master masons and their crews, as well as the unskilled labourers on the ground. All building projects of the Middle Ages featured just such an individual, who was essential to their success. It was his task to describe the architect's plans to workmen unable to comprehend the complex architectural drawings.*

Since Battista d'Antonio, for all his practical experience, had no formal training or theoretical preparation in building design, it was necessary to appoint someone else who would serve, in effect, as the architect-in-chief rather than merely the leader of the works staff. So it was that on the same day that Battista was appointed, the Four Officials, the wardens and the Wool consuls took the extraordinary step of appointing two more *capomaestri*. Filippo's delight in finally being allowed to oversee the project he had been dreaming of for so long must have been tempered by the fact that Lorenzo Ghiberti was appointed as his fellow *capomaestro*. Henceforth the two rivals would be forced to work in close collaboration with each other on the project, sharing a rather meagre salary of 6 florins per month.

This plan surely tempted fate, given Filippo's response to the result of the Baptistery door competition two decades earlier. But Filippo had invested too much time and ingenuity in the project to decline the offer in a fit of pique. This time he accepted his position and then carefully bided his time, aware that he alone, and not Lorenzo, a man with no architectural experience, knew how the dome would be built.

A fourth architect was also appointed, a sixty-year-old humanist philosopher named Giovanni da Prato, who was made deputy to Lorenzo Ghiberti. Giovanni was, among various other accomplishments, the lecturer on Dante at the University of Florence. No sooner did he become

---

* It was from these sorts of communications that, centuries later, the freemasons – a secret society having nothing to do with architecture – would develop their rituals. Many of their secret signs of recognition, for example, are borrowed from the system of words, signs and touches that Hiram of Tyre, the master mason of Solomon's Temple in Jerusalem, was said to have used in order to communicate with the vast army of workers under his command.

involved in the project than he began nourishing a lusty hatred for Filippo. The root of this hatred was a vision of the dome that differed quite drastically from Filippo's. In 1420 Giovanni da Prato was already agitating for a change in the cupola's design because he believed that it would result in a church that was *oscura e tenebrosa* ('murky and gloomy') due to the lack of windows. But his proposed plan that twenty-four windows be incorporated into the base of the dome (a structurally dubious scheme) received little attention from the Opera del Duomo: he was paid 3 florins for his advice, which was then completely ignored. Over the years this rejection would fester in Giovanni's breast and finally lead him to launch several remarkably vitriolic attacks on Filippo.

Three months after these appointments were made, the wardens and the Four Officals of the Cupola made an even more momentous decision: they met to approve a written specification outlining the structural details of Filippo's 1418 model, which they now adopted as the one showing the best method of vaulting. This document is a twelve-point memorandum that describes the dimensions of the two shells, the systems of ribs and chains, the building materials to be used, and so forth. It also mentions the intention to vault without centring, stating that both shells are to be built *sanza alcuna armadura* ('without scaffold-supported centring'), though how exactly this was to be achieved the document fails to state.

Although the author of this memorandum is not known for certain, it seems safe to assume it is Filippo's brainchild.[4] Still, Filippo was not named as the winner of the competition: the Opera did not see fit to award the prize of 200 florins to him or to anyone else. This must have rankled Filippo given that his brick model was to become the new touchstone for the dome: it was put on display in the open air of the Piazza del Duomo, near the campanile. Like the model of Neri di Fioravanti, which still stood inside the cathedral, it was to become a shrine of sorts and would occupy this spot for the next dozen years, with a fence erected around it in order to foil vandals. But Filippo seems to have accepted the Opera's decision not to award him the 200 florins. After all, he was finally to get the chance to vault the dome using his revolutionary techniques.

Men Without Name or Family

THE MORNING OF 7 August 1420 began with a small celebration held 140 feet in the air. The stone-cutters, masons and other labourers on the building site climbed to the top of the tambour of Santa Maria del Fiore, high above the city, and ate a breakfast of bread, melons and Trebbiano wine paid for by the Opera del Duomo. This small feast marked a historic occasion. After more than fifty years of planning and delay, construction of the great dome of the cathedral was ready to begin.

For the previous few months the building site had been a hive of activity. One hundred fir trees, each 21 feet long, had been ordered for the scaffolds and platforms, and the first of almost a thousand cartloads of stone had been delivered. Peering over the edge of the tambour the workmen could have seen spread below them in the Piazza del Duomo scores of these sandstone beams, as well as hundreds of thousands of bricks stacked high.

Life on the building site would not be an easy or an enviable one. The pay was low, the hours long, the work dangerous and the employment sporadic due to bad weather. Most workers in the building trade came from poor families, the *popolo minuto*, or 'little people'. The unskilled labourers — men who carried the lime or bricks — were known as *uomini senza nome e famiglia*, 'men without name or family'. Altogether as many as 300 men worked on the dome, including those in the quarries.[1] Their week was a long one, running from Monday to Saturday, often from dawn to dusk, which in the summer could mean a fourteen-hour day. Payment came every Saturday, when the foreman, Battista d'Antonio, issued the men with chits, or *scritte*, which were redeemed from the pay clerk of the Opera. If fortunate, they might be dismissed an hour or two early, giving them time to buy their food in the stalls of the nearby Mercato Vecchio, which, like everything else, was closed on Sundays. All work was forbidden on the sabbath and during religious feasts, though an exception was made for the men whose job it was to water the masonry on feast days in order to keep it moist and therefore workable. The spreading of manure over the walls – a common method used in the Middle Ages for keeping the masonry moist and protecting it from the elements – does not appear to have been employed at the cathedral. One reason for this might have been that, for reasons of hygiene, it was illegal to import manure into the city.

Religious feasts offered the masons what must have been a welcome relief from their work. On these days they would march in procession through streets swept clear of prostitutes and moneylenders or else make pilgrimages in search of the indulgences sold in stalls along the Via San Gallo. Their most important festival was the eighth of November, the feast of their patron saints, the Quattro Coronati: four Christian sculptors martyred by the Emperor Diocletian for refusing to carve a statue of the pagan god Aesculapius. On this day the men would hear a Mass together, then take food and drink – the latter sometimes to excess, for the guild's statutes state that some of the men conducted themselves on this solemn occasion *come se fussino alla taverna*, 'as if they were in a tavern'.

Taking the sabbath and these religious feasts into account, a full-time labourer could expect approximately 270 days of work on the dome each year, though in fact because of the weather he would probably work a good deal less, perhaps as few as 200. When it was too cold, wet or windy for anyone to work on the summit, the names of all the masons would be put into a leather pouch and Battista d'Antonio would draw those of five men, who were set to work in the shelter, plastering or bricklaying, while the rest of the workers were sent home without pay. Longer layoffs were also a possibility.

These were the uncertain conditions, then, in which the masons would set off for the cathedral each working day. Church bells rang in every district of the city to rouse them from their beds and summon them to their labours. They carried their own tools, which the Opera expected them to supply themselves: chisels, T-squares, hammers, trowels and mallets, all of which could be repaired or sharpened by a blacksmith who operated a forge on the site. Upon arriving at the cathedral the men had their names inscribed on a gesso-board, rather like punching a clock in a factory, while the working hours were recorded by a sand hourglass. Filippo appears to have been a strict master. Later he would institute an even more precise form of discipline on the building site of Santo Spirito, where an *oriuolo di mezz'oro*, a half-hour clock, regulated the working day by chiming every thirty minutes. The conception of time was changing in the fifteenth century. Throughout the Middle Ages it had been associated with the liturgical hours. The Latin word *hora*, or 'hour', was in fact synonymous with prayer. Each of these hours had been divided into four parts of ten minutes' duration, while each minute was divided into forty 'moments'. By 1400, however, it had become the custom to divide the hour into sixty minutes, and each minute into sixty seconds. The pace of life was increasing.[2]

Besides their tools, the men also carried their food with them in leather pouches. The noon meal, the *comesto*, was taken at eleven o'clock, when the church bells sounded a second time. We know that the *comesto* was normally eaten aloft because in 1426, in order to foil idlers, the Opera decreed that no mason could descend from the dome during the day. This must have meant that even on the hottest summer days the workers did not enjoy their *dolce far niente*, or 'sweet idleness', the afternoon siesta when all labours would usually cease because of the scorching temperatures. It was also in 1426 that, on Filippo's orders, a cookshop was installed between the two shells of the cupola in order to serve a noon meal to the workers. The dangers of an open fire on the dome were possibly mitigated by the fact that the masons also served as Florence's firemen. This responsibility fell to them because they owned the tools used to combat fires in the only way that was practical: tearing down walls to create fire-breaks.

To slake their thirst on sweltering summer days the workers drank wine, which they carried in flasks along with their tools and lunches. Strange and inadvisable as a draught of wine might seem under these circumstances, whether diluted or not, wine was a healthier drink than water, which carried bacteria and therefore disease. And the Florentines placed great faith in the wholesome properties of wine. Drunk in moderation, it was said to improve the blood, hasten digestion, calm the intellect, enliven the spirit and expel wind. It might also have given a fillip of courage to men clinging to an inward-curving vault several hundred feet above the ground.

The stonemasons eating their breakfast on the tambour that historic August morning would have needed a good deal of courage. Below them they could see the newly completed vault of the south tribune where, just three weeks earlier, a stonemason named Donato di Valentino had fallen a hundred feet to his death. Another man had also died in the rush to finish the tribune so that work on the dome could begin in the summer. The Opera had paid for both funerals, but this was the extent of the charity that the men could expect. Anyone injured on the job would face a grim future, as would his family, because neither the Opera nor the Masons Guild made provisions for either disabled workers or the widows and children of dead ones. The only social obligation of the members of the Masons Guild was attendance at one another's funerals.

Present in the minds of the stonemasons must also have been the awesome and abiding fact that none of them yet knew whether the structure could actually be erected according to Filippo's plan. Certain details of the cupola's design had been established, of course, in the twelve-point building programme adopted the previous month. The width of the inner dome, for example, was to taper like that of the Pantheon, diminishing from seven feet at its base to just under five feet at the top. And the exterior shell – added to protect the inner one from the elements as well as to make the entire structure appear *più magnifica e gonfiante* ('larger and more inflated') – was to narrow from a width of slightly over two feet at its base to one just over a foot at the oculus. Likewise the eight vertical ribs at each corner of the octagon were to taper as they rose skywards. And while the dead load of the Pantheon had been lessened by the use of pumice-stone and empty bottles, in Santa Maria del Fiore the shells were to be built out of stone for the first 46 feet, then from either brick or tufa, the latter being a light, porous stone formed from volcanic ash. The building programme also outlined, albeit vaguely, the incorporation of a number of rings of sandstone beams held together with cramps of leaded iron – the chains that Neri di Fioravanti had envisioned encircling the dome's circumference. These would be embedded in the masonry and, therefore, hidden from view.

It was the twelfth point that raised the most doubt. The wardens agreed that for the first 30 *braccia* of their height – that is, for a distance of about 57 feet above the drum – both shells were to be built without any scaffold-supported centring. Thereafter, from 30 *braccia* upwards, the dome was to be built 'according to what shall then be deemed advisable, because in building only practical experience will teach that which is to be followed'.

This vital condition reveals the reservations of the wardens in the face of Filippo's daunting plan. Acceptance of it represented a concession on Filippo's part, a means of appeasing the nervous wardens by committing himself to building only the first fifth of the dome without centring. If he succeeded, he would then have to make his case to raise the rest of the cupola in similar fashion. He must have felt frustrated by the wardens' continuing lack of faith, but he may also have felt relieved that he was given some time to consider his plans. It is conceivable that even he was unsure of himself at this early stage. Uncertainty about how to execute his audacious plan, and not simply fear of someone stealing his ideas, may have been one of the reasons why he refused to divulge to the incredulous wardens the secret behind the procedure of vaulting without centring. As late as the summer of 1420, for example, he had still to work out the design of the circumferential stone chains. He would not in fact devise a plan for the first one until June of the following year, barely a month before its construction was due to begin. And plans for the second were not completed until 1425, when yet another model had to be made.

Neither Filippo's brick model of the dome nor the cupolas he built for the two chapels could quite have prepared him for the task ahead. It had long been known that architectural models were poor guides to statics, because what worked structurally in a model could not necessarily be achieved when the proportions were magnified. In the Middle Ages and Renaissance, proportionally identical models behaved differently depending on their respective sizes, and scale models were generally misleadingly strong.*

Given the experimental nature of Filippo's plan, the 30 *braccia* limit seems to have been a wise precaution, especially since a sound logic governs the restriction. At a height of 30 *braccia* the bed joints of the masonry would have risen to form an angle of 30 degrees to the horizontal, or just inside the critical angle of sliding.[3] Friction alone would keep the stones in place up to an angle of 30 degrees, even when the mortar was green; therefore, no centring would have been required until that point. Above that level, however, each course of masonry would incline more sharply, reaching a maximum angle, near the top, of 60 degrees to the horizontal. No doubt it was impossible for the wardens to imagine how these courses might be held in place without centring of some sort.

Both Filippo and the wardens seemed to be purchasing themselves a

---

* Vitruvius describes the problem in an anecdote about an engineer named Callias who designed a model of a revolving crane which was to be set on the walls of Rhodes and used to capture enemy siege engines. The model itself functioned perfectly well but the enlarged version did not, forcing the Rhodians to resort to the old-fashioned method of pouring rubbish and excrement over the heads of their besiegers. Nor were such difficulties in scaling up designs limited to ancient or medieval times. In the late 1980s the Pentagon encountered just this problem when it expanded one of its successful designs – the Trident intercontinental ballistic missile – only to discover that the end product, the Trident 2 missile, had the flaw of triggering its own self-destruct mechanism four seconds after leaving the water.

little time by deferring the central question of how the dome should be vaulted. All were agreed that, in an unprecedented structure like the dome, any constructional difficulties could be solved, as the 1420 programme stated, only by means of 'practical experience'. This was perhaps to err on the side of optimism. But just such a process of trial and error was about to begin.

Some Unheard-of Machine

I am accustomed, most of all at night, when the agitation of my soul fills me with cares, and I seek relief from these bitter worries and sad thoughts, to think about and construct in my mind some unheard-of machine to move and carry weights, making it possible to create great and wonderful things.

These words are spoken by the statesman Agnolo Pandolfini in a philosophical treatise written by one of Filippo's ablest disciples, the architect and philosopher Leon Battista Alberti. *Della tranquillità dell'animo* ('On the Tranquillity of the Soul') was composed in 1441, a few years after Filippo's dome had been completed. It features a dialogue between two men who have suffered miserably from changes in fortune: Agnolo, who has retired, disillusioned, from public life, and a younger man, Nicola de' Medici, whose bank has failed, leaving him destitute. Their conversation takes place inside Santa Maria del Fiore, under the new dome, and concerns the various means of overcoming depression. Agnolo lists a number of traditional remedies for raising the spirits, such as wine, music, women and sports. But his most effective tactic, he tells Nicola, is to fantasise about the construction of giant hoists and cranes that can be used to create 'great and wonderful things' – machines for raising magnificent structures, that is, like the dome that swells above them.

One of the most obvious problems in building the dome of Santa Maria del Fiore – or indeed any large structure – was how to transport heavy building materials such as sandstone beams and slabs of marble several hundred feet above the ground and then place them into position with the accuracy demanded by Filippo's design. The sandstone beams weighed some 1,700 pounds each, and hundreds of them needed to be raised on to the cupola. To solve this problem Filippo was compelled to imagine 'some unheard-of machine' to move and carry tremendous weights to incredible heights. The hoist that he created was to become one of the most celebrated machines of the Renaissance, a device that would be studied and sketched by numerous other architects and engineers, including Leonardo da Vinci. And it was also, no doubt, the inspiration behind Agnolo's soothing fantasies.

A number of machines were already in use on the building site, of course. Twenty years earlier a *rota magna*, or 'great wheel', had been constructed to raise the heavy stones used in the façade, drum and tribunes of the cathedral. This machine, still operational in 1420, was a treadmill that winched loads aloft under the motive power of several men who walked around, hamster-like, inside a large wheel. Such devices had been in use since ancient times. In *De architectura* the Roman architect Vitruvius describes a treadmill turned by 'tramping men', presumably slaves. The treadwheel, a sort of giant spool, either wound or unwound a rope that, in passing through a system of pulleys, raised or lowered the weight attached to its end. The muscular effort involved in powering these winches was not excessive provided the loads were relatively light and the heights to which they were transported not especially high.

Recognising that the *rota magna* would be woefully inadequate to the task of lifting heavy stones to the height required by the dome, the Opera del Duomo had specifically called for models of lifting devices in the 1418 competition. But the models submitted in the ensuing months showed only the cupola or its centring rather than the machines for their construction. Two weeks after the appointment of the three *capomaestri*, the Opera was still referring in its documents to an intended plan of using a plain treadmill – possibly the old *rota magna* – for hoisting the materials. Filippo must have found such a lack of enterprise appalling. He eagerly responded to the challenge and, in one of his first acts as *capomaestro*, began designing a machine that would be powered not by men but by the busiest and most prized beast of burden in the Middle Ages, that powerful but placid creature, the ox.

Work on this new hoist started in the summer of 1420. For its parts Filippo contracted with a wide number of artisans, many of them from outside Florence. Several weeks after the celebratory feast on the tambour, the Opera received shipment of an elm tree from which the drums for the new hoist were to be hewn. The tree must have been enormous, because the largest of the three drums was five feet in diameter. Elm was chosen for its resistance to the elements, for clearly the hoist would need to be in service for many years. Other parts for the hoist had also begun arriving: chestnut poles for the building of the supporting frame and a harness and reins for the oxen. A rope was ordered from Pisa, a shipbuilding town where the art of rope-making was highly advanced. Still, Filippo's hoist must have taxed even rope-makers accustomed to fitting out the largest galleons, for it required one of the longest and heaviest ropes ever manufactured: 600 feet long and weighing over a thousand pounds.[1]

Construction on the hoist continued throughout the winter of 1420–21. A blacksmith was engaged to make bearings for the pulleys of the hoist and a turner to cut cogs from ash wood for its wheels. Meanwhile a barrel-maker began making hoisting tubs to hold the loads of masonry and mortar on their ascents. Finally, two master carpenters were hired to build the frame and assemble the various parts. Each of them spent sixty-seven days on the job.

Work must have proceeded at a furious pace, because in the spring of 1421 the hoist took its place on the floor of the octagon. Or rather it took its place on a 29-foot-long wooden platform specially constructed for the oxen that were to make thousands of revolutions over the next dozen years. Before the dome was complete the hoist would raise aloft marble, brick, stone and mortar weighing an estimated 70 million pounds.

8. A drawing by Taccola of Brunelleschi's ox-hoist, in this case being driven by a horse. At the bottom, the helical screw which raises and lowers the wheels is clearly depicted.

Filippo's ox-hoist was remarkable both for its sheer size and power, and for the complexity of its design, especially its reversible gear, an important innovation for which there is no known precedent in the history of engineering. In the words of one commentator, the machine was 'centuries ahead of the technical understanding of the time'.[2] It consisted of a wooden frame, fifteen feet in height, to which were attached a number of horizontal and vertical shafts or spindles that rotated each other by means of cogged wheels of varying sizes. The machine was set in motion by either one or two oxen yoked to a tiller that turned the vertical shaft. This shaft or rotor was furnished with two cogged wheels, one at the top and another at the bottom, either of which could mesh with a much larger wheel on a horizontal axis. Only one of the wheels on the rotor could be engaged at a time, however: one to raise loads, the other to lower them. The change in gears was effected by a large screw with a helical thread. Turned in either direction, it would lift or drop the rotor several inches, thereby engaging one or other of its pinions with the teeth of a wheel attached to the *sùbbio grosso*, the largest of the three rope drums.

This screw that raised and lowered the rotor was one of the hoist's most ingenious features. It served as a clutch, connecting or disconnecting the two gears from the wheel of the large drum. This meant that the hoist could be reversed – and loads either raised or lowered – without the driver being forced to unyoke the oxen and turn them round. The oxen, that is, only ever moved in a clockwise direction. The obvious benefit of this gear change was that a great deal of time was saved between each ascending or descending operation. Oxen were ideal for moving heavy loads, given their stamina and strength. But they could not be made to walk backwards more than a few steps, a reluctance that hampered any driver trying to unyoke them from the tiller.

When one of the two pinions on the vertical shaft was in mesh with the cogs on the horizontal shaft, the gear train was set in motion. The large rope drum was attached to a medium-sized horizontal spindle, the *sùbbio mezzano*, which, through a secondary set of gearing at its opposite end, engaged another shaft, the *sùbbio minore*, a smaller horizontal spindle

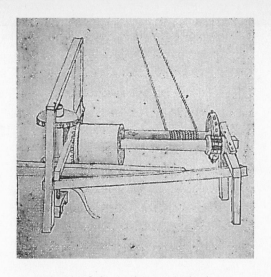

9. A detail of the ox-hoist which shows, on the right-hand side, the secondary set of gearing.

running parallel with the two other rope drums. Any of these three horizontal shafts — small, medium or large — could be used to raise or lower loads. Because of their varying diameters, however, each turned the rope at a different rate of speed and required a different degree of effort from the oxen. The *sùbbio grosso*, five feet in diameter, raised the load more quickly than the *sùbbio minore*, which was only 20 inches in diameter and therefore forced the oxen to make many more revolutions for each ascent. This smallest shaft was used to raise the heaviest loads, much in the same way that a cyclist uses the smallest chain wheel to engage the bicycle chain on steep ascents. Using this shaft, one ox could raise a load of 1,000 pounds to an elevation of 200 feet in approximately thirteen minutes.[3]

Once inaugurated in the summer of 1421, the giant hoist must have been a marvel even in Florence, where the building boom of the previous fifty years meant the populace was accustomed to seeing machines raising skywards heavy loads of brick and stone. After being transported in a cart from the quarry to the building site, a sandstone beam weighing almost two tons would be slid into the octagon on elder-wood rollers that had been greased with tallow or soap. It was then attached to the hoist rope by means of a special hanger, the sort of mortise-and-tenon contrivance now known as a 'lewis bolt'. This hanger was yet another of Filippo's innovations, probably inspired by his study of Roman masonry.

It required a rectangular hole a foot long to be cut into the top of the stone, then undercut several degrees such that it was dovetailed, narrowest on the surface and widest at the bottom. Next, the three iron bars comprising the hanger were inserted into the hole. The outside two were dovetailed in order to fit the mortise, while the middle one was flat. The outside bars were inserted first and then prevented from slipping out of the socket by the middle one, which would have been hammered into place, providing a tight fit. Finally, a crossbolt was slid horizontally through the eyes in the top of the three bars and the rope attached to it. The stone was then ready to be winched on to the cupola.

Certain perils were inherent in the operation of the ox-hoist. Friction had to be minimised because the energy lost in friction created heat, which could easily start a fire, an obvious catastrophe if the beam was dangling in mid-air. And Filippo's enormous rope, with its cross section of some two-and-a-half inches, would have been in danger of combustion, for thick ropes with a great resistance to bending generate a lot of friction. Smooth walnut tubes were therefore used to encase the drums, and the rope was wetted with water in order to prevent it catching fire as it passed through the pulley wheels. Sea water, vinegar or spoiled wine were preferable to fresh water, which rotted the rope.

Once the load reached the working level, a signal was shouted from the cupola and the oxen were halted. The rope was detached from the crossbolt and, far below, the clutch screw was turned, changing the gear. The oxen trudged forwards again, unspooling the rope from the drum, which now rotated in the opposite direction, bringing the rope back down to the floor of the octagon, where it would be attached to another lewis bolt that in the meantime had been secured to the next sandstone beam. The whole operation would then begin all over again. It must have run like clockwork, for the hoist raised, on average, fifty loads per day, or roughly one every ten minutes.[4]

The exact inspiration for this remarkable machine remains as mysterious as that behind Filippo's other inventions. The specialist theoretical knowledge needed for constructing such a hoist was largely unavailable in 1420, though soon afterwards a number of manuscripts on Greek mechanics and mathematics began arriving in Florence, putting architects and inventors of the Renaissance in possession of engineering techniques far beyond those available in the Middle Ages. In 1423, two years after Filippo finished building his hoist, a Sicilian adventurer named Giovanni Aurispa returned from Constantinople with a hoard of 238 manuscripts written in Greek, a language that scholars in Italy had learned only in the previous few decades. Among these treasures were six lost plays by Aeschylus and seven by Sophocles, as well as works by Plutarch, Lucian, Strabo and Demosthenes. But there was also a complete copy of the works of the geometer Proclus of Alexandria and, even more important for engineers, a treatise on ancient lifting devices, the *Mathematical Collection* of Pappus of Alexandria. This latter work, from the fourth century AD, describes the windlass, the compound pulley, the worm and wheel, the screw and the gear train — all essential features of hoists and cranes. In the decades that followed, so many manuscripts on Greek mathematics and engineering emerged that it is possible to speak of a 'renaissance of mathematics' in fifteenth-century Italy.[5]

All of these discoveries came too late to help Filippo with his ox-hoist. In any case the *capomaestro*, like Shakespeare, knew little Latin and less Greek, so these manuscripts would have been of slender value to him unless they were first translated into Italian.* Filippo therefore probably knew about the workings of pulleys, clutches and gear trains not through old parchments but, rather, from his own experience. Growing up only several hundred yards from the cathedral he saw in almost daily operation what Manetti calls 'a variety and multitude of different devices': treadmills and cranes built under the direction of previous *capomaestri*, including Giovanni di Lapo Ghini, who in the 1350s devised a treadwheel for winching masonry to the vaults of the nave. Still, however much they may have stimulated Filippo's youthful imagination, these machines would have

---

* That Filippo read no Latin — or very little, at any rate — is known because of the fact that in 1436 Alberti translated *De pictura*, his work on perspective, into Italian so that his master could read it.

been unsophisticated in comparison to the ox-hoist, consisting simply of shafts and wheels that moved a rope over a system of pulleys. It is unlikely in the extreme, for instance, that any of them included complex meshing parts such as those featured in his own hoist, let alone prototypes of the motion-reversing clutch.

Manetti also suggests another inspiration for the ox-hoist. He claims that Filippo, while still a young goldsmith, built a number of mechanical clocks equipped with 'various and diverse generations of springs'. If this story is true, these devices would have been as far ahead of their time as the ox-hoist. All mechanical clocks during this period were driven by a falling weight attached to a cord spooled round a drum. As the weight descended it unwound the cord and turned the drum, which then rotated a wheel whose teeth — like those on the wheel of the ox-hoist's *sùbbio grosso* — engaged the pinions and gears of the driving-train, the motions of which were regulated by an escapement. But Filippo's clocks, according to Manetti, used springs instead of weights to drive their gear-trains — an astonishing claim, since spring-loaded clocks are not known to have been invented for almost another hundred years. Indeed, elastic springs of the sort needed for such clocks were not developed until many decades later, when metallurgical techniques were refined enough that it became possible to manufacture resilient wire.

Apart from Manetti's claim, no evidence exists for these spring-driven clocks other than an anonymous sketch done later in the century, possibly based on a design by Filippo's friend Mariano Taccola, who is known to have drawn a number of the *capomaestro*'s inventions. It is plausible, however, that Filippo's experimentations with clock mechanisms, with cog-wheels and counterweights, served him when the time came to design his ox-hoist.[6]

Whatever its inspiration, the hoist inspired great confidence from the start. As soon as it was finished, Filippo pressed the Opera for a prize, mindful that no one had so far received the 200 florins promised in the 1418 proclamation. Within a month a substantial award of 100 florins was granted to him 'for his ingeniousness and labours in connection with the device newly invented by him for hoisting'. In what now seems like a

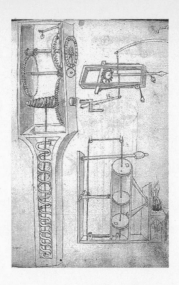

10. A drawing of a spring-driven clock, possibly based on one
of Brunelleschi's designs.

classic understatement, the Opera commended him for the design of this
hoist, 'which is more useful than the one previously employed'.

The ox-hoist had been designed to raise heavy loads far into the air with
maximum speed and efficiency. In this task it probably excelled any hoist
ever constructed, for one or two oxen were able to raise loads that before
had taken as many as six pairs. But this remarkable machine none the less
shared the shortcoming of all hoists: devised only to raise or lower
burdens, it was unable to move them laterally. Yet sideways motion was an
obvious requirement for laying the beams for the stone chains. These
beams were interlocking and, at several levels, radially tilted towards the
vertical axis of the dome. A machine capable of shifting them infinitesimal
distances in any direction – up, down or sideways – was therefore required
so they could be laid in place with pinpoint accuracy.

Since 1413 a crane known as the *stella* had been used for the vaulting of the tribunes. But ten years later this machine, like the *rota magna*, was no longer adequate for the greater demands of the cupola. A more powerful crane with a longer working arm was needed. And the Opera del Duomo met this challenge in typical fashion: it proclaimed yet another competition, asking for designs to be submitted by April 1423.

The winter of 1422–3 proved to be a hard one. The *tramontana*, a raw wind that, according to folklore, brought depression and fatigue to Florence, howled down from the Apennines. In January work on the cupola stopped because of the cold and a network of boards had to be placed over the walls to protect them from snow. Filippo took advantage of this hiatus in order to devise a crane for the competition. Given the success of the ox-hoist, the result of the Opera's deliberations could have surprised no one: in April the wardens selected his design over one submitted by a rival, Antonio da Vercelli, whom Vasari implies was a creature that Lorenzo Ghiberti thrust forwards in the hope of challenging Filippo's expertise and thwarting his authority.

Within a few days the wood for Filippo's machine began arriving at the building site: eight pine beams, along with two elm trunks, each 15 feet long. Then a walnut tree was delivered from which the crane's screws would be carved. As with the ox-hoist, the machine was built in a remarkably short time, less than three months, and was ready by the beginning of July.

Known as the *castello*, this new crane consisted of a wooden mast surmounted by a pivoted horizontal beam. Sitting high on the cupola, it must have resembled a gallows. The horizontal crossbeam was furnished with screws, slideways and a counterweight. One of the horizontal screws moved the counterweight along the slideway, while the other manipulated the load, which could also be raised or lowered by means of a turnbuckle. This turnbuckle permitted the installation of the stone with far greater control than the ox-hoist, whose driver, several hundred feet below, relied on shouted commands from the cupola.

The *castello* would go into operation as soon as the ox-hoist delivered the stone to the working level. Standing on a small platform at the top of the

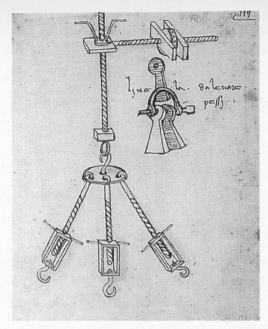

11. A drawing by Buonaccorso Ghiberti of three turnbuckles and, inset, a lewis bolt to attach a piece of stone to a hook.

crane – one of the giddiest and most dangerous of all of the stations on the cupola – the operator turned the horizontal wooden screw that moved the load laterally through the air beneath the crossbeam. At the same time, the counterweight at the other end of the beam was adjusted in order to keep the crane in equilibrium. A horizontal arm projecting from the mast prevented the load from swinging at the end of the rope – a danger in the high winds that swirled round the cupola. Then, once the stone was hovering above its final destination, the turnbuckle was adjusted and the load descended into place.

The success of the *castello* is remarkable given the lack of understanding of the strength of materials at the time. Other than through precedent, Filippo had no way of knowing the robustness of his crane's long horizontal beam when placed under the stress of a heavy load. Not until the studies of the French engineer Claude-Louis Navier in 1813 was the bending strength of beams mathematically determined. In 1420 calculations

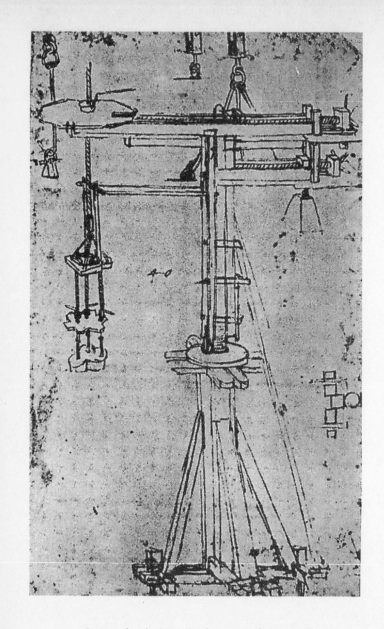

12. Leonardo da Vinci's drawing of the *castello*.

were based on ancient theories about the various 'humours' of trees in the same way that the medicine of the day – equally suspect – was concerned with the interaction of humours in the body. Elm, for example, the wood used in the crossbeam, was said to be 'dry', therefore it did not 'agree' with the plane tree or the alder, which were 'moist' and so ought never to be used in the same structure as elm – a most dubious set of assumptions on which to rest a sandstone beam weighing over 1,000 pounds. The sight of one of these heavy stones dangling at the end of a crossbeam must have been, initially at least, an unnerving sight.

But the crossbeam held and the *castello*, like the ox-hoist, needed only minor repairs in the decade that followed. Indeed, in one respect the *castello* was to prove *too* durable. Like the ox-hoist, it remained on the cathedral's building site through the 1460s, long after Filippo's death, and was present during the last act of the dome's construction: the placement of the eight-foot-high bronze sphere that sits atop the lantern. The commission for this bronze ball went to the sculptor Andrea del Verrocchio, in whose workshop there was at this time a young apprentice named Leonardo da Vinci. Fascinated by Filippo's machines, which Verrocchio used to hoist the ball, Leonardo made a series of sketches of them and, as a result, is often given credit for their invention. How Filippo would have reacted to this misattribution – Filippo, who was so proud of his inventions and so fearful of plagiarism – scarcely bears contemplation.

The Chain of Stone

N O SOONER WAS the ox-hoist finished than plans began moving ahead for the first sandstone chain, and in early June a design for the chain had finally been settled upon: a carpenter working for Filippo, a man named Jacopo di Niccolò, was paid for a wooden model demonstrating how the beams would be linked. This chain was complex in design, consisting of two concentric rings of stone laid horizontally around the octagonal circumference of the dome. These long beams rested on, and interlocked with, shorter beams laid transversely, like railway sleepers, at intervals of every three feet. Before June was out, some eighty-six cart-loads of sandstone had arrived in the Piazza del Duomo from the Apennines.

Seen from either the dome or the campanile of Santa Maria del Fiore the hills surrounding Florence have the sensuous contours of a supine body. Dozens of quarries were worked on their slopes during the Quattrocento, including several near the village of Settignano, the childhood home of Michelangelo, whose wetnurse was the wife of a stone-cutter and, according to the sculptor, the source of his genius with hammer and chisel. The hills are formed from *macigno*, a quartz-bearing sandstone so hard that during the Middle Ages it was favoured for grindstones. In Florence it was also used in the construction of buildings. So abundant were its seams that all one had to do to build a house

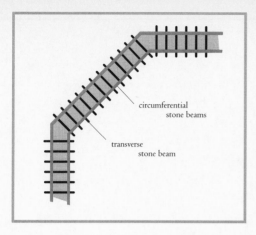

circumferential
stone beams

transverse
stone beam

13. The sandstone chain.

in Florence, it was said, was to dig a hole and then pile up the stones. Several quarries were actually found within the city gates, between the convent of Santa Felìcita and the Porta San Piero in Gattolino (now the Porta Romana); one of them was even owned by the convent's nuns. The Arno also provided the city with supplies of stone: a limestone known as *lapidum Arnigerum* was quarried along its south bank. But the stone for the circumferential chains would come from the Cava di Tras-sinaia, a quarry a few miles north of the city, near the ancient town of Fiesole. Work sheds were erected on the site in March 1421, and soon afterwards a team of nineteen stonemasons went to work.

Most stonemasons served their apprenticeships in the quarries, learning from their masters how to recognise the best beds of stone, how to cut with or against the grain, and how to dress them according to the architect's templates. The extraction and shaping of a stone made for strenuous labour. A saw was first of all used to cleave the stone from the hillside. In the case of a hard stone like *macigno*, mixtures of sand and iron filings would be sprinkled under the teeth of the saw to act as abrasives and compensate for the comparative softness of the metal. Prised free with a crowbar and wooden wedges, the stone was cut roughly to size with a pickaxe and afterwards dressed using a hammer with a lighter blade. It was then sounded as a test of its quality – that is, struck lightly with a hammer. If there were no flaws, the stone would ring like a bell, whereas a dull thud indicated a crack or some other defect, and it would be discarded. Another test of quality was the smell. Freshly cut from a quarry, limestone and sandstone smell of rotten eggs, and the stronger this sulphurous stench, the better the quality of stone.

The dimensions and shapes of the stones needed for Filippo's chains were highly particular. Each of the long circumferential beams had to be $7\frac{1}{2}$ feet long and 17 inches in section. Furthermore, each stone was to have a series of notches cut into its underside so it could interlock with the shorter beams laid transversely beneath. The first sandstone chain used over a hundred of these long beams and almost as many of the short ones.

Templates, either drawn on parchment or carved from wood, were used as guides for dressing the stone. But because of the complexity of Filippo's design, the stonemasons had difficulty understanding how exactly the stones were to be cut and then fitted together. The enterprising *capomaestro* therefore made other, less conventional models for them to follow. A number of these were made from wax and clay, and some he even carved from *rape grandi*, large turnips that the Florentines ate in winter.

To function effectively the circumferential stones, which met at 45-degree angles, needed to be linked tightly together at their ends. This was achieved by iron clamps that coupled them together. Filippo travelled to Pistoia to oversee the casting of these clamps, which were so specialised that the ironmongers, like the stonemasons, could barely understand what was required of them. Once forged, these clamps were glazed with lead to prevent the iron from rusting and therefore causing the surrounding masonry to crack. Many thousands of pounds of lead were used for rustproofing both these clamps and the iron bars installed elsewhere in the cathedral. Plumbers (whose name comes from the Latin *plumbum*, 'lead') were employed at most cathedrals in the Middle Ages in order to rustproof iron or make lead tiles for the steeples. Such a recourse, naturally, meant one more danger for the workers at Santa Maria del Fiore, for it had been known at least since the time of the Romans, when the architect Faventinus observed the 'deformity' and 'dreadful anaemic pallor' of plumbers, that lead was a poisonous metal.[1]

The sandstone chain was only the first of four to be laid, part of a system of four bands that would encircle the dome at regular intervals of 35 feet. In the spring of 1425 Filippo executed a model for the second chain, which was even more complex than the first because the transverse beams were radially disposed, like a set of spokes, towards the vertical centre or 'hub' of the dome. Also, they were inclined at an angle rather than laid horizontally, a process that would require the expertise of the new *castello* as well as, we shall see, an extremely precise system of measurement.

The Opera's documents record that the sandstone beams were to be superimposed by continuous iron chains. Iron has a far higher tensile strength than sandstone, meaning that the iron chains encircling the dome would actually have provided most of the resistance to the horizontal thrust. However these chains, so essential to the dome's success, are also one of its secrets: it is impossible to know their composition, for the simple reason that all of them are embedded in the masonry and therefore hidden from view. There is no reason to assume that they were not installed, but a magnetic survey conducted in the 1970s failed to detect any evidence of them.

The sandstone chains are not the only circumferential ties in the dome. They were supplemented by a fifth, made of wood and installed in 1424, which encircles the dome 25 feet above the first stone chain. Four of these wooden chains were originally planned, but in an example of how 'in building only practical experience will teach that which is to be followed', only the first was ever executed.

The wooden chain created problems for Filippo from the start. The programme of 1420 had specified that it should be made from beams of oak 20 feet in length and a foot wide. But a year later, when sufficient quantities of oak proved hard to find, chestnut was chosen instead. In all, twenty-four beams would be needed, three on each side of the octagon, and they would be spliced together with clamps made from oak. Although the chestnut beams were ordered in September 1421, as the first sandstone chain was being laid, they would not arrive until more than two years later

— no doubt a discouraging sign to anyone still dreaming of erecting the structure with a large wooden centring. There was, first of all, the problem of finding chestnut trees of an adequate diameter. Then, once the timber was found, it had to be felled in accordance with various rules and traditions, such as waiting for the wane of the moon, since wood cut at this time was thought less apt to breed worms. And once felled, it had to be properly seasoned, a time-consuming operation. First of all, its sap was driven off by soaking the wood in water for up to a month. Alternatively, the timber would be buried for several weeks in ox dung, in much the same way that animal hides were tanned with manure. The wood was then placed on a bed of ashes or bracken and exposed to the air, but protected from the rain and sun, for anything up to several years. Given these various procedures, it is little wonder that Filippo faced such a wait.

Like the four stone and iron chains, the wooden chain was no doubt part of Filippo's system of invisible buttressing, a means of containing the hoop stress of the dome, for wood, like iron, has a greater tensile strength than sandstone. It may even have been intended to protect against a particularly violent kind of stress. A similar series of wooden ties were incorporated into the base of the dome of Santa Sophia in Constantinople, at the point where the greatest tension would develop, while more timber bonds were introduced into the brickwork following the earthquake of AD 557.[2] Likewise, a double ring of poplar beams embraces the dome of the tomb of Öljeitü at Sultaniya, put there to counteract damage caused by the earthquakes on the Plateau of Persia.

Did Filippo have a similar form of protection in mind when he designed his wooden chain? Manetti alludes to 'hidden devices' that were placed inside the dome to protect it from both the wind and earthquakes. Wind loading (the force exerted on the dome by the wind) was not of particular consequence, because of the sheer size of the structure.[3] Earthquakes, on the other hand, were a factor. Quakes would strike the city in 1510, in 1675, and again in 1895. The shocks from the first of these were so severe that many people spent the ensuing nights camped in the open air of the piazzas rather than returning to their homes. None of these earthquakes, however, caused damage to the cupola.

There may also have been another reason for the timber chain: a political rather than a structural one. It appears to have been, at least in part, an elaborate intrigue on the part of *capomaestro* Brunelleschi, a means of undermining the authority of Lorenzo Ghiberti by exposing his ignorance in matters of architecture and engineering. For, several years into the building of the cupola, the battle between the two *capomaestri* was about to explode.

The Tale of the Fat Carpenter

THE RIVALRY BETWEEN Filippo and Lorenzo had been simmering for several years. Although the two men had been appointed as equals, Filippo had swiftly eclipsed Lorenzo. After the ox-hoist was built and the first stone chain laid, he was referred to in the documents as the *inventor et ghubernator maior cupolae*, a title indicating how he had risen above his colleagues. Filippo's mandate, according to the wardens, was to 'provide, arrange, compose or cause to have arranged and composed, all and everything necessary and desirable for building, continuing and completing the dome'. Lorenzo, by contrast, was merely to 'provide' towards this end. So it must have irritated Filippo to know that Lorenzo was not only enjoying the same salary – 3 florins per month – but likely to share the credit for Filippo's ingenuity.

The wooden chain afforded Filippo the opportunity of discrediting his colleague. Models for this chain had been designed by Filippo as well as by the two other men, including Giovanni da Prato. A prize of 100 gold florins was at stake. In August 1423 Filippo's design was selected by the wardens, yet another victory for the *capomaestro*, whose reputation was looming ever larger. But when the chestnut trees finally arrived in Florence, disaster seemed to strike: Filippo took to his bed, complaining of a pain in his side. He lingered there for several days, and when he was finally induced to return to the building site he did so only with his head bandaged and his chest poulticed. This theatrical display managed to convince many people that Filippo was at death's door. Others believed he was malingering, and soon rumours were bruited about Florence that his mysterious illness was actually a lack of nerve, an inability to follow through on his grandiose and impossible plan. The invalid made no response, merely shuffling back to his sick-bed.

Responsibility for building the wooden chain – and for raising the dome – therefore fell to Lorenzo. This enormous obligation caused the goldsmith no small amount of disquiet, for Filippo, true to his nature, had not made his colleagues privy to the structure of the wooden chain, let alone the ultimate design of the dome. But it was Filippo's model for the chain – one as confusing to the uninitiated as all of Filippo's models – that Lorenzo suddenly found himself charged with reproducing.

Work on the site ground to a halt as the stonemasons and carpenters awaited their instructions. Filippo was requested to return to the site and offer his advice. But the condition of the *capomaestro* was deteriorating so swiftly that great alarm was aroused in the Opera. Finally, afraid of exposing his ignorance, Lorenzo bade the men resume, and under his direction they began laying the chestnut beams along one of the eight walls and fastening them together.

Interconnecting these logs was an important and complicated task. Lorenzo proceeded in this operation as best he could, basing his design on the wooden chain that embraces the dome of the Baptistery. But Filippo's model called for a more complex design in which the logs would be clamped together with special plates made from oak. These had to be attached both above and below the junctions of the logs by iron bolts. The logs would then be wrapped in iron straps to prevent the bolts from splitting them.

As soon as three beams had been connected along one wall, Filippo made a miraculous recovery. He rose from his deathbed, spryly ascended into the cupola, inspected Lorenzo's work and then began a whispering campaign against Lorenzo, declaring his oak fastenings worthless and claiming that all three logs would have to be removed and replaced with a more effective construction – one that was ultimately executed under his own supervision. Thus, whatever its structural function, the wooden chain ultimately became a means for Filippo to expose Lorenzo's incompetence to both the wardens and the people of Florence.

Filippo found himself rewarded for this intrigue a short time later: his salary was almost tripled, to 100 florins per year. Lorenzo's remained at 36 florins until the summer of 1425 when his pay was suddenly suspended. No further wooden chains were built. But if Filippo thought he had subdued Lorenzo and his deputy, Giovanni da Prato, he was sorely mistaken.

If Filippo's illness was indeed feigned, it was not the first time he had played an elaborate trick on an unwary party. He was well known in Florence for his talents in mimickry, chicanery, theatricality and the creation of illusions. His most famous bit of trickery was a complex and ingenious hoax perpetrated against a master carpenter named Manetto di Jacopo. The story, known as 'The Tale of the Fat Carpenter', gained the status of legend in Florence and is related by Filippo's biographer, Antonio Manetti.[1] An example of a *beffa*, a cruel and humilating trick, it is worthy of the pen of Boccaccio and anticipates the topsy-turvy dreamworld into which the characters are plunged in Shakespeare's *A Midsummer Night's Dream*.

The hoax took place in Florence in about 1409, during one of Filippo's returns from Rome. The victim was a carpenter named Manetto, known as *Il Grasso*, or the 'Fat Man'. Manetto specialised in carving ebony and owned a shop in the Piazza San Giovanni, not far from Filippo's house. He was prosperous and good-natured, but one day had the misfortune of incurring Filippo's ire after missing a social gathering. Never one to resist retaliation, Filippo resolved to exact his revenge for this perceived slight by persuading a wide cast of characters to convince Manetto that he had metamorphosed into someone else: a well-known Florentine named Matteo.

As Manetto closed his shop one evening, Filippo went to his house near the cathedral, picked the lock, slipped inside and barred the door behind him. When Manetto arrived a few minutes later, he rattled the door and then, to his alarm, heard what sounded like his own voice (in fact, Filippo doing an impersonation) ordering him to go away. This impersonation was so convincing that he retreated in bewilderment into the Piazza San Giovanni. There he met Donatello, who inexplicably addressed him as Matteo, and shortly afterwards a bailiff, who likewise hailed him as Matteo and then promptly arrested him for debt. He was taken to the Stinche prison, where his name was entered in the gaol book as Matteo. Even his fellow prisoners – all of them party to Filippo's prank – addressed him by this alien name.

The carpenter spent a sleepless night, fretting over events but solacing himself with the thought that he was merely a victim of mistaken identity. This comfort evaporated the next morning when two strangers – the brothers of the real Matteo – arrived at the prison and claimed him as their kin. They paid his debt and liberated him, though not before chastising him for his supposed gambling and profligate living. More bewildered now than ever, he was escorted to Matteo's home on the other side of Florence, near Santa Felicita, where his protests that he was not Matteo, but Manetto, appeared to fall on deaf ears. Over the course of an evening he almost became convinced that he had indeed metamorphosed into someone else. He was then put to sleep with a potion supplied by Filippo and carried, unconscious, back across the river to his own home. He was laid on his bed in a reversed position, with his head at the foot and his feet at the head.

Awakening many hours later, the poor carpenter was confused not merely by his position on the bed but also by the disarray of his house, for his tools had been completely rearranged. His perplexity grew with the arrival of Matteo's brothers. These two men now treated him differently, greeting him as Manetto and relating the curious story of how the previous evening their brother Matteo conceived the fantastic notion that he was someone else. The story was soon confirmed by Matteo himself – the real one – who arrived at Manetto's house to describe his puzzling dream of having been a carpenter. The disarray of the house was explained by the fact that in his dream Matteo noticed how his tools were out of order and in need of rearrangement. Faced with this evidence, Manetto became more convinced than ever that, for a while at least, he had exchanged identities with Matteo – in the same way that their names, so close in spelling, could be shuffled together and confused.

This practical joke confused art and life in the same manner as the perspective panel that Filippo would paint a few years later. Just as he showed the viewer of the painting a clever fabrication that tricked him into mistaking the artificial for the real, he fashioned a unique perspective for Manetto by reordering and controlling his perceptions. Like the viewer peering through the peephole, Manetto could not know whether what he experienced was the 'real scene' or only a convincing but none the less distorted mirror image of that reality. Coincidentally, the perspective panel, which featured the Piazza San Giovanni, may even have included a representation of Manetto's shop. By that time, however, the unfortunate carpenter had left Florence, humiliated and confused. After the trick was exposed, Manetto emigrated to Hungary, where he successfully plied his trade and – in what makes a happy ending to the story – amassed a considerable fortune.

10

The Pointed Fifth

IN AD 148 THE ROMAN hydraulic engineer Nonius Datus was sent to the town of Saldae in Algeria and instructed by its governor to build an aqueduct through the middle of a mountain. Nonius duly surveyed the mountain, executed plans and cross-sections, calculated the axis of the tunnel and then supervised two gangs of experienced tunnellers as they began their excavations, each at a different end. Thereupon he returned to Rome, satisfied that the operation was progressing smoothly. Four years later, however, he received an urgent summons to Saldae. Upon arriving he discovered the population of the parched town in a despondent mood: the two teams excavating the tunnel had each accidentally deviated to the right and therefore failed to meet in the middle. Nonius managed to rectify the situation, but had he arrived a little later, he observed, the mountain would have possessed two tunnels instead of one.

This anecdote is related in *On Aqueducts*, a work written by Sextus Julius Frontinus, the chief water engineer of Rome and one-time governor of Britain. Lost for many centuries, the treatise was discovered at Monte Cassino in the 1420s by the manuscript-hunter Poggio Bracciolini. The tale of Nonius and his errant tunnellers must have been a source of chastening reflection for the builders of the cupola, who had been faced with a similar constructional problem — that is, how would it be possible for eight teams of masons, each working on one side of the dome, to raise their separate walls so that they would all converge at the top?

One of the keys to raising the dome was the precise calculation and measurement of each horizontal layer of brick or stone as it was added in a gradually contracting sequence. But how would these measurements be taken? How could the curvature of the eight individual walls be controlled during the process of construction? The difficulty was made even more acute by the fact that each wall had to incorporate two shells rising in tandem, as well as their supporting ribs. A deviation of only several inches in one of these ribs — each of which was over 100 feet in length — meant that the connection, like that at Saldae, would not be achieved.

The teams of masons at work on the dome had certain basic measuring devices at their disposal. Most of these had not changed significantly for a thousand years. For checking the perpendicularity of walls, for example, they used plumb-lines: a string on which a weight, usually a ball of lead, was suspended. The string would be braided like a fishing line in order to prevent the weight from rotating in the breeze. And to ensure the stones were laid in perfectly horizontal courses or layers, a mason's level was employed. This instrument was shaped like the letter A: a plumb-line hung from its apex, while the horizontal cross-piece was inscribed with a graduated scale. The plumb-line would come to rest in the centre of the cross-piece when the stone or brick was on a level plane.

As they are neither perpendicular nor horizontal, vaults such as arches and domes obviously demanded a more complex system of measurement. The master builders of the Gothic cathedrals regulated the curvature of such structures by first plotting them full-scale, like a giant set of blueprints, on to special tracing-floors. These floors were covered in plaster of Paris on to which life-sized geometrical designs of, say, a vault's ribs would be drawn. Once these drawings were complete, carpenters used them to devise the wooden templates from which the stone for the ribs was shaped by the masons working at the quarry. The gypsum floor was afterwards wiped clear and the next set of drawings incised into its surface. If facilities for tracing-floors did not exist, an area of ground would be cleared and the designs sketched in the soil. In 1395, for example, the plan for the timber trusses of the roof at Westminster Hall were set out on a patch of ground near Farnham in Surrey.

It was this latter method to which Filippo resorted in the summer of 1420. Downstream from Florence he had a large area of the Arno's bank levelled, an expanse roughly half a mile in every direction, and in the sand he traced a full-scale plan of the dome.[1] It is most likely that the templates for each of the eight vertical ribs were made from this enormous geometrical design. These models, cut from pine, were $8\frac{1}{2}$ feet in length and roughly 2 feet wide. Sheets of iron were used to stiffen them and prevent their warping. They were fitted on to the outside wall of the inner shell, allowing them to serve as guides for both shells, which were built with identical inclinations. Moved progressively upwards as the dome rose, they ensured that the eight massive ribs would ultimately converge at the level of the fourth stone ring. In order for these ribs to serve as guides for the rest of the dome's vertical curvature, they were built first: that is, only after several courses of the bricks for the ribs were laid did the masons begin filling in the intermediate sections.

Regulating the curvature of the ribs was not the only problem that confronted Filippo and the master masons. The cupola's bricks were not laid in horizontal courses but rather at ever increasing angles to the horizontal plane, with the final layers leaning inwards at a steep 60-degree angle. A method therefore had to be found of guiding and controlling this gradual inclination. A related difficulty was calculating the radial dispositions not only of the bricks but also the transverse sandstone beams of the second and third stone chains: all of this masonry had both to tilt inwards as well as to radiate from the vertical centre of the dome. Under such circumstances, traditional tools such as plumb-lines and mason's levels were quite useless.

How exactly Filippo calculated the disposition of the bricks and the massive stone beams is another of the dome's mysteries. However, in *Historia florentinorum*, written sometime during the 1490s, the humanist poet and historian Bartolomeo Scala offers a hint as to how he might have done it: 'For, when the centre [of the dome] was pinpointed and marked,' Scala claims, 'Filippo stretched a cord from the centre to the circumferences. Carrying on this process around in a circle, he determined in what order and according to what curvature the bricks and mortar were to be placed on the wall by the masons.'

That is, in order to guide the laying of the bricks, Filippo ran a cord (what the documents call *corda da murare*, or 'building string') outwards from the centre of the dome to the inside edges of the masonry. This cord, which could be swept 360 degrees around the cupola, would have risen and then progressively shortened as more courses of bricks were added and the dome's radius shrank from 70 feet at its foot to only 10 feet at the top. The inclination of the bricks as well as their radial positionings could therefore have been carefully monitored.

Scala's account is supported by Manetti, who claims that Filippo used this same procedure when vaulting the Ridolfi Chapel. In this experiment the *capomaestro* used a cane that was fixed at one end and 'circled upwards, gradually narrowing as it pressed constantly on the bricks on its unfixed side'. This device anticipates the modern-day 'trammel' used by bricklayers in order to set out circular walls. The trammel consists of a horizontal wooden plank that pivots on an upright metal bar fixed at the centre of the wall's curvature. Describing an arc as it rotates round this axis, the plank indicates the position in which each individual brick should be laid.

Still, the curvature control device at Santa Maria del Fiore was obviously a much larger instrument: if it was to stretch from the centre of the dome to its circumference, the *corda da murare* must have been 70 feet long at least. This unwieldy size would have presented certain problems. How, for example, was the cord prevented from sagging in the middle and therefore causing inaccurate measurements? Was a system of pulleys used? Or was it tautened and then smeared with wax like the ropes used by surveyors in the Middle Ages?

But most perplexing is how the cord was fixed at the dome's centre. A wooden pole would have had to have been 180 feet high to reach from the ground to just the base of the cupola, and almost 300 feet high to reach its top. The average height of a mainmast for a ship in the British Navy during the eighteenth century was 120 feet, and such masts could be built only with wood from the forests of the New World – Quebec, Maine and New Hampshire – since no trees of sufficient height were to be found anywhere in Europe.[2] As one commentator has observed, 'One would have to fantasise an enormous trunk of a California sequoia hoisted onto a central tower or suspended platforms'.[3]

Whatever Filippo's method of controlling the curvature of the dome, it had its critics. Not surprisingly, the most insistent of these came from the camp of Lorenzo Ghiberti. Late in 1425 Lorenzo's deputy, Giovanni da Prato, appealed to the wardens that Filippo was failing to observe the terms of the 1367 model. As *capomaestro*, Filippo had of course sworn his allegiance to this sacred structure, just like all of the *capomaestri* before him. Yet Giovanni was dissatisfied. He voiced a number of complaints, the most serious of which was a claim that Filippo was not building the cupola according to the proper profile, the *quinto acuto* or 'pointed fifth' curvature established by Neri di Fioravanti.

This pointed profile was important to the cupola both structurally and aesthetically. The pointed arch was, of course, the favoured Gothic method of spanning space: the arches in the nave of Santa Maria del Fiore are pointed, for example, as are those in the naves of most Gothic churches. The pointed arch has two distinct advantages over the rounded or semicircular one that would come to dominate architecture throughout the Renaissance. The first has to do with proportions, for a pointed arch rises higher than a semicircular one of equivalent span. In 1367 this factor no doubt influenced the thinking of the wardens of Santa Maria del Fiore, for a dome with a pointed profile was able to stand as much as a third higher than a semicircular one built over a tambour of equal diameter. Only with a pointed curvature, that is, could the cupola reach the desired height of 144 *braccia*.

The second advantage of a pointed arch is structural. The horizontal thrust of an arch or dome varies inversely with its rise, and since a pointed arch rises higher than a rounded one it naturally generates less thrust. In fact, the architects at the Cathedral of Milan believed that pointed arches produced no horizontal thrust whatsoever. They were mistaken, of course, though a *quinto acuto* arch does generate as much as 50 per cent less radial thrust than a shallower, semicircular one. It therefore requires less abutment and has a lower tendency to crack or burst at its base.

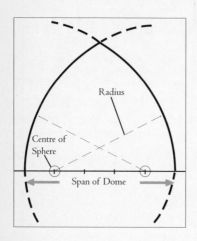

14. The *quinto acuto* arch.

The *quinto acuto* profile demanded in 1367 is a geometrical figure produced when the radius of curvature in the intersecting arches is four-fifths of the resulting span. The radius of curvature in a semicircular vault, by contrast, is only one half the diameter, leading to a much shallower and more rounded profile. It was this figure about which Giovanni da Prato raised the alarm. In a submission to the Opera del Duomo he maintained that the dome had been 'falsely built' because Filippo was constructing it 'half round' and not as the specified pointed fifth. It was being built, that is, as a *mezzo acuto*, halfway between a semicircular arch and a pointed fifth. The result would be a dome incapable of reaching the required height. And Giovanni attributed this error not to some fault in the system of curvature control but, instead, to Filippo's ignorance.

'I, the aforesaid Giovanni,' he wrote with some indignation, 'declare that it seems to me that the angle chosen and suggested decades ago ought not to be changed or modified by lowering it for any reason whatever.' The dome would be aesthetically marred otherwise, he insisted, not to mention structurally unsound. In short, Filippo's error in deviating from the established curvature would 'brazenly spoil and endanger the church'. This submission ends, unsurprisingly, with a bitter personal attack on Filippo:

Dante reading from the *Divine Comedy* in front of Santa Maria del Fiore

A fifteenth century panorama of Florence

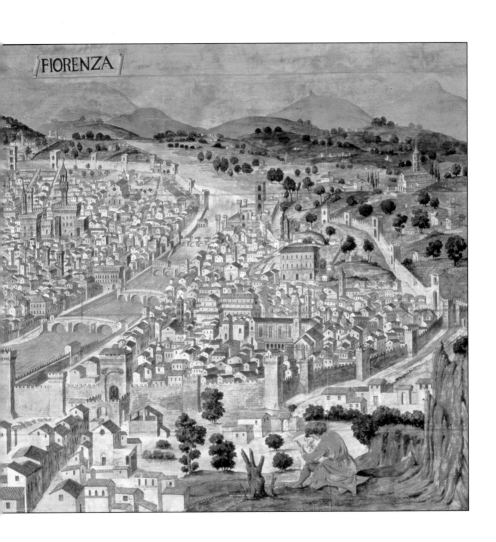

A view of the belltower and cathedral

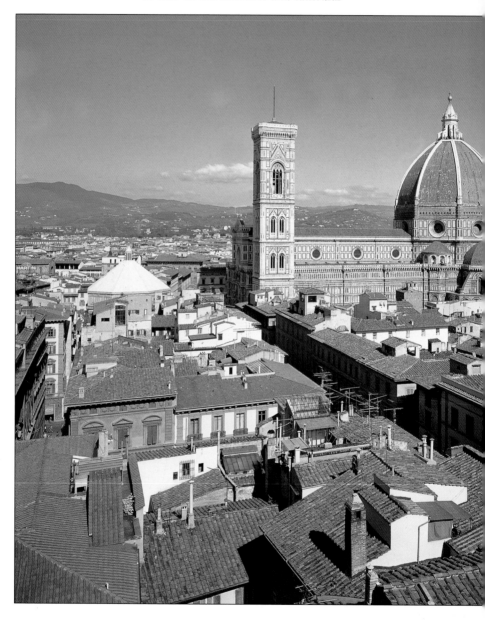

The buttresses and ribs of the dome seen from the lantern

The interior of the dome with Vasari's fresco

The air space between the two shells of the dome with the
herring-bone brickwork visible in the bottom right-hand corner

This has happened because of ignorance and presumption on the part of those to whom the execution has been entrusted, and who are being well paid and compensated for it. And I have written this so that if it befalls which all reason tells me must befall, and the building is spoiled and put in danger of ruin, I shall be excused and blameless. For God's sake, be prudent, which I am certain you will be. Think of the danger that befell the cathedral of Siena for trusting a dreamer incapable of reasoning.

The tone is that of a biblical seer predicting future calamities should his words go unheeded. The unfinished extension to the cathedral of Siena to which he refers was a gargantuan folly that was partially torn down in 1357 after plague struck and funds ran out — a catastrophe that had for obvious reasons haunted the minds of the builders of Santa Maria del Fiore.

The motives behind Giovanni's submission to the Opera were not perhaps the purest, especially since there was no basis for his claims. The shells, as built, conform exactly to the specified *quinto acuto* profile, and no corrections appear to have been necessary at any point during the construction.[4] The fact that Giovanni was so mindful of his own reputation ('I shall be excused and blameless'), as well as so obviously resentful of the fact that Filippo was 'well paid and compensated' for his work, leads one to suspect a motive of jealousy.

In 1425 Giovanni had good reasons to be jealous of Filippo, even though he was himself an accomplished man, a respected humanist scholar who had composed a famous philosophical treatise, the *Paradiso degli Alberti*. However, like Lorenzo he had thus far failed to make an impression in the field of architecture. Filippo's model for the wooden chain had been selected over one of his own, winning the *capomaestro* the very substantial prize of 100 gold florins. In the same year Filippo also won the competition for the design of the *castello*. Meanwhile, of course, his ox-hoist had been a great success and the sandstone chains, the second of which was being laid in 1425, were working according to plan. Filippo's reputation, in short, had never been better. To complete his triumphs, a few months earlier Lorenzo Ghiberti had been suspended from his duties as *capomaestro*, possibly because of Filippo's intrigue involving the wooden chain. He would be reinstated shortly afterwards, albeit with reduced responsibilities and powers. The Ghiberti faction had reached its lowest ebb.

Giovanni da Prato's submission to the Opera del Duomo did not end with complaints about the curvature of the dome. His document returned to his earlier obsession with light in the cathedral, complaining that, lit only by the eight windows in the tambour, as well as by the oculus at the top, the cathedral would be made 'murky and gloomy' inside. To prove his point, he drew a section of the cathedral showing how a beam of sunlight entering one of the windows in the drum would be insufficient to illuminate either the cupola above or the crossing below.

The illumination of a church was an important architectural consideration. Gothic builders had sought to fill their churches with plenty of light by designing enormous windows filled with stained glass, but the merits of 'light' or 'dark' churches were matters of considerable debate during the Renaissance. Alberti, for example, argued that churches should be dark inside, lit only by candles and lamps. But Giovanni's complaint about the murkiness of Santa Maria del Fiore was to be echoed over a century later in Rome when Michelangelo, taking over the construction of St Peter's, criticised the previous *capomaestro*, Antonio da Sangallo, for designing a dome that would render the cathedral so dark inside that nuns would be raped and criminals concealed.

In Giovanni's view there was only one way to save Santa Maria del Fiore from darkness: he urged the wardens to dust off and reconsider his old, rejected plan in which twenty-four windows were to pierce the base of the cupola and thereby fill the church with glowing light. His tone became hectoring and apocalyptic: '*Per dio uogliate pro uederui,*' he begged them ('For God's sake, take care of it'). Once again he sought to absolve himself of any responsibility should things go wrong: 'I have written this in order to be blameless if nothing should be done about this problem.'

But Giovanni's pleas again fell on deaf ears. In the amendments made to the cupola project in January 1426, Filippo wrote: 'We make no special suggestions regarding the light because the illumination from the eight windows below seems to be adequate.' He added that if it should be discovered that more light was required, then windows could be incorporated at the top of the dome – a solution already angrily rejected by Giovanni as one that could only be advanced 'by a fool of small understanding'. It was evident that the Opera sided with Filippo rather than Giovanni, because construction proceeded on the cupola as before, with the same curvature and without windows at the base; and several weeks later Filippo received his salary increase to 100 florins per year. Giovanni, meanwhile, was paid 10 gold florins for his advice, after which he remained on the periphery of the project.

But this debate was not the last that Filippo would hear of Giovanni da Prato. Soon afterwards the *capomaestro* began work on another invention, one which would enjoy far less success and esteem than any of his previous ones, and Giovanni would have his revenge.

Bricks and Mortar

ESPITE HIS SUCCESSES in the early years of the dome's construction, Filippo must have been dogged by the knowledge that once the dome reached a height of 30 *braccia* the wardens would meet again to consider whether or not to continue building without centring. Early in 1426, after the second sandstone chain had been swung into place, that moment arrived. The dome had risen to 70 feet above the drum, and the shells, curving inwards, had passed the critical angle of 30 degrees, above which friction alone would no longer keep the masonry in place until the mortar cured.

In contrast to the furore when Filippo first floated his plan, in 1426 the debate over whether to continue building the dome without centring appears to have gone smoothly. The *capomaestro*, now at the height of his powers, carried the day: 'We still do not recommend centring,' the amended project reported, citing the difficulties of building the necessary scaffolding. But it remained to be seen whether this feat could successfully be accomplished.

The documents of February 1426 give no more than the merest hint how Filippo's plan would be implemented. At the same time that it was decided to vault the rest of the dome without centring, another amendment was adopted: in certain parts of the cupola a series of uniquely shaped bricks were to be laid in a special fishbone bond. The twelve-point memorandum of 1420 had decreed that after the two shells reached a height of 24 *braccia*, either brick or tufa stone should replace sandstone to lighten the load. Brick was ultimately chosen because tufa was not readily available in the vicinity of Florence and so needed to be imported. The Opera therefore contracted for hundreds of thousands of bricks, and Filippo began designing special wooden moulds in order to shape them.

The size of bricks was carefully regulated in Florence.[1] The basic brick used in the construction industry, the *mattone*, was about 10 inches long and 5 inches wide. All brickyards were required to display the mould for this brick, stamped with an official seal, where it could be consulted both by their customers and by inspectors from the Masons Guild, who would arrive on the premises wearing distinctive blue capes and silver badges.

The cupola, however, called for bricks of more unorthodox designs: rectangular bricks, triangular bricks, dove-tailed bricks, bricks with flanges, bricks specially shaped to fit the angles of the octagon. The sizes of these bricks were so various, and the templates used to design them so numerous, that at one point parchment ran short and Filippo was forced to improvise: he resorted to palimpsests, drawing his designs on pages torn from old books specially bought for the purpose.

These templates were sent to a barrel-maker who constructed the wooden moulds used to shape the bricks. Once the mould was finished, it went to the brickyard. These were normally located in the countryside, not only in order to spare Florence the twin nuisances of fire and pollution, but also to be close to the clay pits as well as the supplies of the timber and brushwood that fuelled the kilns. Dug from the pits, the clay was kneaded into a smooth and even consistency by the exertions of barefoot men, who trod it underfoot like grapes. The resulting 'pug' was then moulded, seasoned and, finally, baked. The firing would last for several days, but because the kiln was heated to a temperature of 1,000 degrees Celsius the brickmaker had to wait almost two weeks for it to cool down enough for the bricks to be unloaded. The average kiln held as many as 20,000 bricks and, fired every three weeks, could bake over 300,000 a year.

Even at this rate, however, it would have taken one kiln over thirteen years to produce enough bricks for the dome.

Manetti claims that Filippo himself inspected each and every brick destined for the dome. This is surely an exaggeration given that as many as four million were used. But quality control was obviously a major concern for the *capomaestro*. Bricks often shrank or cracked during firing because the clay had not been properly seasoned, and shipments were rejected if the consignment was not of the quality required. Ideally the clay was dug in the autumn and, after being moulded, was buried in sand in order to avoid frost damage in the winter. In summer the unbaked bricks were excavated and then reburied in beds of moist straw to prevent them from cracking in the heat. Alberti cautions that a brick must be seasoned for two years before being burned, making for a process as time-consuming as treating timber. Nor was the baking of bricks the cleanest of occupations: a joke in Florence claimed that only kilnmen washed their hands *before* visiting the chamber-pot.

Equally important to the building of the dome was the quality of the mortar, in which Manetti claims Filippo also took a personal interest. Throughout the Middle Ages mortar was made from mixing sand and water with quicklime (calcium oxide), a substance obtained by heating limestone in a kiln. Making mortar for a structure the size of the dome called for enormous quantities of limestone. Most brickmakers burned limestone as well as bricks in their kilns, using a separate furnace for the operation, which took some three or four days. Lime-burning was a noxious process that prejudiced the health of anyone living downwind. It was dangerous for another reason as well, since air pockets in the limestone could cause explosions in the kiln. Air pockets were often the result of fossils, a phenomenon with which stone-cutters, for obvious reasons, had become more familiar than anyone else. These petrified remains were objects of great curiosity: Alberti, in some fascination, describes having seen worms with hairy backs and a great number of feet 'living' inside blocks of limestone.

As we have already seen, the speed with which a mortar set determined the techniques of construction. Medieval mortar set in two phases. The first took place after a few hours, when the material was no longer plastic, while the second was not complete for a much longer period. This second setting required carbon dioxide absorbed from the atmosphere to convert the calcium hydroxide of the mortar paste back into calcium carbonate, the basic constituent of limestone. This is the same chemical reaction that, with greater leisure, creates stalactites on the roof of a limestone cavern, where carbon dioxide turns the calcareous matter in the dripping water back into its native limestone.

Alberti claims it is possible to tell when this second set occurs because the mortar puts forth 'a kind of moss or little flower well known to masons'. It is not easy to know which plant he is referring to, though the most likely candidates are mosses from the *Bryum, Tortula* or *Grimmia* families, all of which grow on limestone walls several months after a mortar is applied. It has been speculated that Filippo may have sped up the process by using a quick-drying mortar, possibly even pozzolana, which would have been a truly remarkable innovation, marking the first use of Roman cement for a millennium. But mineralogical tests conducted in the 1970s revealed no material difference between the mortar in the cupola and that elsewhere in the cathedral. In each case, however, sodium carbonate, or soda ash, was present, a mineral used in glass-making. It would have led, whether intentionally or not, to a fairly rapid stiffening of the mortar.[2]

Mortar was always mixed on the site. The process took about a day since if the quicklime was not well slaked – that is, thoroughly mixed with water – it would damage the brickwork. The mixing was done on the cupola itself because it needed to be applied while still plastic. Lime, sand and water were all hoisted to the top of the dome, where the lime was slaked and then combined with the sand. Slaking generated great heat and caused the quicklime to expand and then disintegrate into a powder. One of the perils involved in mixing the mortar was burning one's hands on the quicklime, a corrosive substance otherwise used to hasten the decomposition of corpses and so lessen the stench and danger of disease in churchyards. It was also employed by tanners to scorch the hair off animal hides.

Once properly mixed, the mortar was poured by the masons on to their mortar boards and, in time-honoured fashion, spread over the brickwork with trowels. Each of the eight teams of masons laid its bricks on the inside of the wall and worked outwards, with the bed joints of successive courses inclining as the structure rose. Both shells were raised simultaneously, with the inner built to a thickness of 6 feet, a width of over ten bricks. The outer shell, much thinner, was a third that size.

Work advanced at a slow pace because the eight teams of masons were forced to wait until each ring gained strength before they began a new one. The average rate of construction has been estimated at less than one course per week,[3] meaning the cupola would have risen at a rate of roughly a foot each month. Erecting the dome with a centring would have demanded a much more rapid construction because of the tendency of the wood to deform or 'creep' over time. But a structure the size of the cupola could not possibly have been built swiftly enough to avoid this deformation – yet another reason for vaulting without centring.

The adhesion of the bricks was not Filippo's only worry at this point. These were dangerous times for the teams of masons, who now had to work on walls that leant inwards at an alarming angle. A dome built with a wooden centring had a comforting network of scaffolding to break a fall and obscure the view of the abyss. In this case, however, there was nothing: the masons simply moved around the perimeter of the cupola on *ponti* (narrow platforms made from willow withes and supported on wooden rods inserted into the masonry) while below them yawned the chasm. In order to pacify the nervous masons, Filippo built a *parapetto*, or balcony, on the inside of the vault. This contraption consisted of a series of boards erected on hanging scaffolds projecting from the masonry. A platform much wider than the *ponti*, it served both as a safety net and – even more vital – as a screen. According to the documents, it was intended 'to prevent the masters from looking down'.

Other safety measures were also implemented. Masons working high on the walls were given leather safety harnesses, and their wine was to be diluted with a third part of water, a mixture normally reserved for pregnant women. Anyone violating this latter rule was subject to a fine of 10 lire, or the equivalent of eleven days' work. Workers were also forbidden to transport their tools, lunches or, worse still, themselves in the tubs of the hoist. Nor were they permitted to swing inside the hoisting tubs in order to capture pigeons nesting in the cupola. Nesting pigeons were a perennial nuisance to masons. During the construction of Westminster Abbey, canvas sheeting had to be used to keep them from taking up residence among the stones and beams of the half-finished structure. The pigeons so daringly captured by the masons at Santa Maria del Fiore before the edict took effect were probably destined for the dinner pot. Blackbirds also met this fate, for meat was a rare luxury for workmen, being eaten for the most part only on Sunday.

These various safety measures appear to have worked: after the two deaths in the south tribune in the summer of 1420, only one other fatality is recorded, that of a mason named Nenno di Chello who fell to his death in February 1422. It is an almost miraculous safety record considering the number of men employed, the perilous nature of their work and the many years the project took to complete.

Another hazard faced by the masons was unemployment. As the shells rose and the circumference gradually narrowed, fewer bricks needed to be laid and therefore fewer masons were needed. Twenty-five of them were sacked in April 1426, though in this case the redundancies may have resulted from a labour dispute. Manetti claims the master masons 'selfishly unionised themselves' – an act contrary to Florentine law – and went on strike for higher pay. Conflict over working conditions may also have played a part in the strike. Such strikes were not unknown in Florence, where the all-powerful guilds were reluctant to extend liberties to the workers upon whose toils their own prosperity depended. The previous century had seen strikes, secret meetings, rock-throwing crowds, the beginnings of working men's associations, even full-scale insurrections.[4] The most famous example of the latter was the so-called Ciompi uprising of 1378, when the city's downtrodden cloth-workers revolted against their masters and, amid mass disturbances, set fire to the palaces of the aristocratic families and temporarily seized control of the Republic.

No such revolution was permitted to erupt at Santa Maria del Fiore. Filippo responded in ruthless fashion, promptly sacking the masons and hiring Lombards to replace them – the strike-breaking technique beloved of later opponents of trade unions. Finding themselves unemployed, the dismissed masons humbly petitioned Filippo for the return of their old jobs. Vasari, who also tells the story, gleefully reports that Filippo did indeed rehire them, but on lower salaries, 'so instead of getting something more, as they thought they would, they suffered a loss, and in venting their spite on Filippo they injured and disgraced themselves'.[5]

It is safe to assume that the masons, like the stone-cutters and ironmongers, were initially puzzled by what the *capomaestro* required of them. It comes as no surprise that the brickwork in the shells was as complex and inventive as everything else Filippo designed for the cupola. The bricks were not merely laid in horizontal layers: at regular intervals in both shells the rings were interrupted by larger bricks laid on their ends – that is, at right angles to the horizontal courses. This angled brickwork is the *spinapescie* (fishbone) bond mentioned in the 1426 amendment. These vertical bricks, each of which passed through four or five horizontal rings, ascended in diagonal bands to the top of the

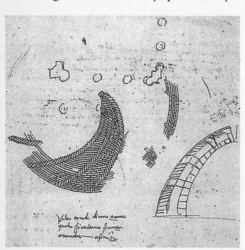

15. Herring-bone brickwork.

dome, forming a zigzag or herring-bone pattern. Filippo must have known that these spiralling bands of upright bricks would constitute planes of weakness, since they were less able than a more conventional bond to counter the hoop stresses that threatened to crack the dome.[6] Why, then, should he have chosen to use the herring-bone bond?

The reason behind Filippo's choice of this pattern lies in the particular structural behaviour of arches and domes. A dome is built on the principle of an arch, whose stones, as we have seen, are kept in place by mutual pressures brought into play by their own weight. Once complete, each of them is under circumferential compression and therefore, like an arch, becomes self-supporting. But the problem in constructing a dome arises from the fact that these rings cannot be built instantaneously. Some form of temporary support is therefore needed until the rings are complete because, until they are closed, the tendency of the masonry is obviously to fall inwards.

Filippo used the herring-bone bricks in order to counter this tendency. The upright bricks projecting from the horizontal courses served as what one of the cathedral's *capomaestri*, Giovanni Battista Nelli, surveying the cupola over two hundred years later, called *morse*, or 'clamps'. From his observations Nelli realised that Filippo had adopted a different pattern of brickwork at the level of the second sandstone chain, as the masonry began curving inwards, and that this pattern had helped to hold in place the surrounding horizontal bricks as the mortar cured. Every three feet or so, these upright bricks interrupt the horizontal courses, subdividing each new layer into shorter sections roughly five bricks long. While under construction, the short sections were connected by the upright bricks to several completed layers beneath. Each row of five bricks, that is, was locked into position by the vertical bricks on either side. These acted rather like book-ends, keying the new layer to the completed, self-sustaining ones beneath.

The incomplete courses of bricks were therefore held in place not by an internal support (as in the case of a wooden centring) but by a pressure applied from either side. Even before the ring was complete and the mortar had cured, the short sections of bricks were transformed into self-contained horizontal arches capable of withstanding the inward pull of gravity. The herring-bone pattern is therefore essential to the dome's structure, an ingenious system used by Filippo as part of his technique to do away with the need for an elaborate centring. In *On Architecture* Alberti later describes this technique as being essential for building a vault without centring, because connections bind the weaker components to the stronger ones. He compares the result to the human body, in which Nature 'joins bone with bones and binds the flesh with tendons, introducing connections in all directions in length, breadth, depth and slantwise'.

Where exactly Filippo learned of the herring-bone bond is one of the dome's unsolved mysteries. The pattern had of course been known to masons and bricklayers for many centuries. The Romans made extensive use of the bond they called *opus spicatum*, and the pattern is also found in the half-timbered brick walls of Tudor houses in England. In both these cases, however, it is decorative rather than structural; indeed, the Romans used it only in ornamental paving on the floors of their villas.[7]

Slightly further afield, systems of interlocking brickwork similar to that in the cupola in Florence can be found in certain Persian and Byzantine domes, leading some scholars to speculate that Filippo may have visited these lands. This hypothesis is not improbable given the trade link with Asia Minor (which was so well known to Italians as early as the thirteenth century that Marco Polo did not consider it worth describing) as well as Filippo's many 'lost years' between 1401 and 1418. He may also have gained second-hand knowledge of these domes from merchants returning from the East or even, possibly, from the many Muslim slaves in Florence. No wealthy family in Florence could do without at least a couple of these 'domestic enemies' (as Petrarch called them), among whom were found Turks, Parthians and Chaldeans, all from the Near East.[8] Still, the majority of these slaves were adolescent girls, and their familiarity with Seljuk vaulting techniques must have been scanty.

Having inspected the dome's brickwork, Nelli was confident that the method could be applied elsewhere, daring to envision other such enormous structures. 'Operating in this manner,' he wrote, 'any massive curved structure can be raised from the ground to any height whatsoever without support from centring or scaffolding.' The dome of another of Filippo's designs, Santo Spirito, was built in this way, and Antonio da Sangallo the Younger made use of it in the next century. But the full magnitude of Nelli's claim has never been tested except at Santa Maria del Fiore. This is for the simple reason that no masonry dome larger than Filippo's great cupola has ever been constructed.

Circle by Circle

THE BOOK OF GENESIS tells us that after the Flood, when everyone on earth still spoke the same language, some of the descendants of Noah travelled east into the deserts of Babylonia, in modern-day Iraq. Hoping to make a name for themselves, these new inhabitants of Babylonia took it upon themselves to found a great city named Babel, or 'the gate of God': *And they said, Go to, let us build us a city, and a tower, whose top may reach unto heaven.*

The rest of the story is well known, of course. It is a parable of the ambitious pride of mankind and, more specifically, of architects. Using kiln-baked bricks mortared together with tar, the people of Babel built an edifice that rose to an incredible height. But the tower was never finished. Angered by man's attempt to reach the heavens — to build beyond his assigned station on earth — the Lord confounded the tongues of the builders so that no one could understand anyone else's speech. Not surprisingly, the ambitious project ended prematurely and unhappily.

Modern commentators speculate that the story of the tower of Babel is an attempt by the ancient Hebrews to account for the enormous, half-ruined ziggurats, or stepped pyramids, that had been raised by the Sumerians, the world's oldest civilisation. The story also seeks to account for linguistic diversity, for we learn that after abandoning their tower, the

Babelites with their myriad new languages were dispersed across the face of the earth, giving rise to new nations, each with its separate tongue. But the story is likewise an architectural version of the Fall of Man. The attempt to reach the heavens, and therefore to rival God, recalls Adam and Eve's ambition to gain forbidden knowledge in the Garden of Eden. The great tower – a would-be bridge between man and God – becomes an architectural equivalent of the Tree of Life, which likewise would have erased the difference between the Creator and his creatures.

Buildings of large dimensions have always posed moral problems.[1] A number of Roman authors disapproved of excessively large edifices either because of their lack of utility or because of the tremendous expenditure involved in their construction. Plutarch, for example, condemned the enormous baths and palaces of the Emperor Domitian, and both Pliny and Frontinus vehemently rejected the Seven Wonders of the World, which the former regarded distastefully as a foolish display of wealth on the part of kings. By contrast, the aqueducts maintained by Frontinus, though immense, served the important purpose of bringing fresh water to the citizens of Rome.

In the twelfth century, the Cistercian abbot Bernard of Clairvaux condemned the vast height of the new Gothic churches that were rising everywhere across France. Such suspicions can also be found in the writings of Leon Battista Alberti, who attacks the pyramids in the same critical vein as Pliny and Frontinus, claiming that the 'monstrous' works of the Egyptians were an 'insane idea'. In light of this pronouncement, his positive estimation of the dome of Santa Maria del Fiore (one of whose virtues, he claims, is its sheer scale) comes quite unexpectedly:

What man, however hard of heart or jealous, would not praise Pippo the architect when he sees here such an enormous construction towering above the heavens, vast enough to cover the entire Tuscan population with its shadow, and done without the aid of beams or elaborate wooden supports?

The reference to the dome's all-encompassing shadow may be an allusion to the pyramids of Egypt, which were said to cast shadows as long as a journey of several days.[2] Alberti justifies the gigantic dimensions of the dome because they reveal both evidence of man's God-given power to invent and the superiority of Florentine commerce and culture. Filippo and his masons even appear to have succeeded where the architects of Babel failed, for the dome towers *above* the heavens, achieving and even surpassing the aspirations of the ill-fated Babelites.

Alberti wrote this famous description of the cupola soon after setting eyes on the half-built structure for the first time in 1428, following his return to Florence from exile. The wealthy Alberti clan had been banished from the city seventeen years earlier, when Leon Battista was only four, and he had subsequently been raised in Padua and Bologna. Later famous for his books on painting and architecture, in 1428 he was known for spectacular feats of physical prowess such as piercing an iron breastplate with an arrow and leaping over the shoulders of ten men in succession. Among numerous other accomplishments he was a horse-tamer and the author of treatises on both the arts of navigation and the manners of his pet dog. He invented a disk to compose ciphers (a sort of prototype of the Enigma machine) as well as an astrolabe to survey the ruins of Rome. No subject seemed to escape his attention: Greek, Latin, law, mathematics, geometry. But he took a special interest in architecture, particularly in Filippo's dome, over the top of which, according to legend, he was able to throw an apple.

For Alberti as for everyone else in Florence, watching the dome rise above the city was the most enduring and breathtaking spectacle of the age. Alberti was probably the most interested and informed of these observers, acting as a reliable eyewitness to what later writers have doubted, namely that the cupola was raised without a wooden centring. And he makes an intriguing observation about this engineering feat, which he says 'people did not believe possible'. A polygonal dome can be constructed without a wooden support network, he claims, only if 'a true circular one is contained within the thickness'.

A century after its construction, the Florentine poet Giovanni Battista

16. A detail from Biagio d'Antonio's *Archangels in a Tuscan Landscape* shows
the dome in the background still under construction.

Strozzi described the dome of Santa Maria del Fiore as having been built
di giro in giro, 'circle by circle'. This expression no doubt alludes to the
technique of bricklaying at Santa Maria del Fiore: the process of waiting
for the mortar of one course of masonry to dry before laying another. But
even allowing for metaphor and poetic licence, it is still a slightly odd
description if we consider that the dome is octagonal and not circular, a
fact apparent to anyone who sees it. The difficulty in raising the dome lay
in the fact that it was *not* circular. So what does Alberti mean when he
speaks of a circular dome contained within the thickness of the polygonal
one, or Strozzi when he says that the dome was built 'circle by circle'?

The herring-bone brickwork, ingenious as it was, would not alone have
been enough to stop the dome collapsing inwards. Filippo's real stroke of
genius was in creating a kind of circular skeleton over which the external
octagonal structure of the dome took shape. That is, the dome was
constructed so that it contained within the thicknesses of its two shells a

series of continuous circular rings. The inner shell of the cupola, as we have seen, is the thicker of the two, measuring between 7 feet at its widest and 5 feet at its narrowest. With these dimensions it was large enough to incorporate into its centre a complete circular vault roughly $2\frac{1}{2}$ feet thick. Rowland Mainstone, the English structural engineer who determined this form following a survey in the mid-1970s, explains that the inner dome was constructed 'as if it were a circular dome . . . but with parts cut away from both the inside and outside to leave the octagonal cloister-vault form'.[3] The herring-bone bond was then used to secure the bricks that protruded forward of this circular ring – that is, those bricks on the inner shell that were not part of the horizontal ring.

The outer shell posed a somewhat different dilemma. With a width of slightly more than 2 feet at its base narrowing to just over a foot at the summit, it would not be possible to incorporate a circular vault within its thickness. How then could it, like the internal shell, be made self-supporting? The problem was a lesser one, in some respects, given that it might have been possible to support the masonry of the outer shell on the back of the inner one by using a small network of centring between the two. But this was not the solution adopted by Filippo.

A clue to the method used to build the outer shell in its upper levels can be found in the amendments made to the cupola project in 1426. As well as referring to the herring-bone bond, these make reference to another brickwork construction, a horizontal arch that would be built on the inside of the dome's outer shell: 'Let bricks be built in the form of an arch for the perfection of the circle encompassing the outer shell, in order that this projecting arch may be complete and unbroken.' The purpose of this arch, the amendment states, was to make it possible 'to bring the dome to completion with greater safety'.

Once built, this horizontal arch must have served its purpose, for in the end the masons built eight more of them, all continuous rings that form part of the octagonal structure of the outer shell. They were observed by the cupola's first surveyor, Giovanni Battista Nelli, though their full importance was not recognised until Mainstone's much later survey. Each one is roughly 3 feet wide and 2 feet high, and they encircle the dome at 8-foot intervals, the first one being found just above the second sandstone chain. Visible in places from the internal walkways, they project at right angles from the inside of the outer shell, connecting the corner spurs to the intermediate ribs. Unlike the stone-and-iron chains, they are not intended to neutralise the lateral thrust, although it is possible that they transfer weight from the outer shell to the inner one.[4] They were a temporary measure, and if they appeared crude or obstructive they were to be dismantled and removed once the dome was finished.

These nine rings served a vital function in building the cupola. They begin at the height – some 36 *braccia* above the drum – above which the shell, curving inwards, had passed beyond the critical angle of 30 degrees. This fact explains why the arch-rings (like the herring-bone courses, which serve a similar purpose) were begun at this level and not at a lower one, where the hoop tension is much greater. They are disposed round the circumference of the shell so that they thicken it at the corners which would otherwise have interrupted what the 1426 amendment calls 'the circle encompassing the outer shell', ensuring that this circle is 'complete and unbroken'. The masonry of the outer shell was thus rendered self-sufficient during the course of its construction and prevented from falling inwards. Yet the rings are almost wholly disguised, being visible only in a few places between the two shells. From the outside the dome looks perfectly octagonal, as demanded by the 1367 model. Once again Filippo, the master of illusion, had exploited the difference between surface appearances and internal reality.

Giovanni Battista Strozzi's description of the dome having been built 'circle by circle' is not only a reference to the method of bricklaying or the series of ascending circles that compose the two shells. It is also an allusion to the *Divine Comedy*, where Dante uses this exact same phrase – *di giro in giro* – to describe Paradise, which is envisioned as a series of nine concentric circles. The comparison of the dome to Dante's Paradise is an apt one for a number of reasons. Filippo was a scholar of Dante, having

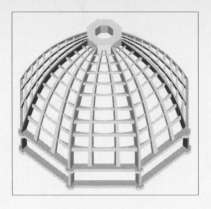

17. The nine horizontal circles within the dome's outer shell.

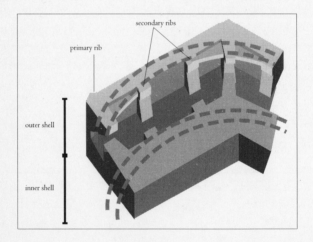

18. A close-up of how the arch rings fit within two sides of the octagon.

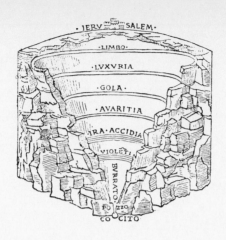

19. Dante's circles of Hell.

made an extensive study of the *Divine Comedy* in which his architectural instincts compelled him to calculate geometrically the precise dimensions of Paradise; and domes have always been a conventional symbol of heaven. In both Eastern and Western art the ceilings of the most revered shelters have been associated with the heavens, visions of which have therefore often been executed on their surfaces in paintings or mosaics. Persian domes were said to express the flight of the soul from man to God.[5]

But the nine arch-rings built by Filippo in the outer shell of his dome recall nine other famous rings: those of Dante's Hell, which is composed of nine rings that descend conically into the earth, rather like an inverted dome. This too is an apt comparison, for in 1428, shortly after the first of the arch-rings was completed, Filippo was to begin his own infernal descent.

The Monster of the Arno

B Y THE SPRING of 1428 work on the cupola appeared to be progressing smoothly. The dome had risen more than 70 feet above the drum in less than eight years, and with the diameter now narrowing it could be expected to ascend even more swiftly in the years to follow. But 1428 would be the year of Filippo's first real setback since work on the dome had begun. His undoing was brought about by what must have seemed a minor problem in comparison with the ones he had already solved.

Over a hundred years earlier it had been decided that every inch of the exterior surface of Santa Maria del Fiore, with the exception of those parts tiled in brick, should be covered with marble. Marble was the typical building material of Antiquity, but it had been used only sparingly in Florence, which was built, as we have seen, primarily from sandstone. Other than for his work on the cupola, Filippo would use no marble at all on his other buildings. Unlike sandstone, marble was scarce in the vicinity of Florence, and transporting it from afar without damaging it was difficult and onerous. Undaunted by these difficulties, the planners of Santa Maria del Fiore had ordered that three colours should encrust the cathedral: the greenish black stone known as *verde di Prato*; the red stone *marmum rubeum*; and, finally, a brittle white marble called *bianchi marmi*. This last stone would cover the eight enormous brick ribs of the cupola, and in June 1425 the Opera del Duomo signed a contract for 560 tons of it.

Bianchi marmi was supplied from quarries near Carrara, 65 miles to the northwest of Florence. The marble from this remote district possesses a long and illustrious history. It was first exploited by the Romans, who used it for the Apollo Belvedere (which would be excavated at Frascati in 1455) and in the Arch of Constantine. Later Michelangelo would carve some of his most famous statues from it, including his *David* and the *Pietà*. In fact, Michelangelo spent a good many months of his life in the steep, dazzlingly white mountains around Carrara, reopening and inspecting old Roman quarries and fantasising about carving gargantuan shapes into the hillsides.

Carrara marble was justifiably the most sought-after in Europe: hard, clean-breaking and a chaste white, it was perfect for carving and ornamentation. It was also extremely expensive. Nevertheless, the Opera had been bringing this white marble to Florence for more than a hundred years, using it, for example, to clad Giotto's campanile. In this enterprise the citizens of the Republic had been conscripted into service: in 1319 the Opera decreed that the people were to lend a helping hand whenever marble for the cathedral was shipped along the Arno. It was to be transported by those who operated small craft, primarily fishermen and the *renaiuoli*, men who scratched a meagre living by harvesting gravel for the building trade from the Arno's numerous sandbanks. This seems to have been an attempt on the part of the Opera to legislate for a sort of 'Cult of the Carts' such as that seen during the twelfth century in France, where the population, gripped by a pious hysteria, helped to drag carts of stone from the quarries to the cathedrals.

The acquisition and working of marble from Carrara was a complex, delicate and occasionally dangerous business. Extraction methods were similar to those for the sandstone at the Trassinaia quarry. Blocks of marble were first of all cut from their mountain beds by roughmasons wielding an array of tools: picks, hammers, crowbars, wedges, even heavy pole-axes to break the larger pieces. Besides brawn, the roughmason required a precise knowledge of the seams and an ability to cut both with and against the grain. After it was rough-hewn into shape, a more skilled artisan cut the stone to the exact size and shape specified by the templates. An even more varied assortment of tools, all of tempered iron, was used in carving the white marble, a stone notoriously difficult to work. A fine-pointed implement called the *subbia* chiselled the block to within an inch or two of the *penultima pelle*, or the second last skin. Then a chisel with a notch in the centre of the blade, the *scarpella*, was used, followed by the *lima raspa*, or roughing file, which came in a variety of shapes and thicknesses.

After these tools had shaped the block into its proper geometrical profile, the surface of the stone was given three or four separate polishes. The first polish involved using an iron plate to rub a sharp sand across the stone, thus removing the irregularities of the surface. The second used a finer sand, or sometimes dust from a whetstone, and the third used rotten-stone, an abrasive red limestone powder known as *tripoli*. The final polish was performed with a putty made from tin oxide. So burnished, the marble would be as smooth as glass.

Dressing the marble at the quarry had the advantage of lower transport costs, for only the finished stone was shipped to Florence, not the heavier and more ungainly rough-hewn blocks. Yet moving the stone intact over long distances and across rough terrains was by no means an easy process. If they passed inspection, the blocks were raised from the quarry with hoisting tackle and conveyed down winding roads on carts – two delicate operations – until they reached the busy town of Carrara, whose cathedral and principal buildings all were built from gleaming *bianchi marmi*. After export taxes were paid, they were carted several more miles to the old Roman port of Luni, on the malaria-ridden coast. Here they were moved across the beach on wooden rollers, lifted on to barges by means of a treadwheel crane, then launched into the waters of the Ligurian Sea. This leg of the journey was particularly perilous, as was discovered in 1421 when one of these barges sank during a storm with a loss of its cargo, a load of *bianchi marmi* destined for the cornice on the dome's rain gutter. After a 25-

mile sea voyage, the boat would reach the mouth of the Arno, up which the cargo was transported over sandbars and shoals towards Florence.

The Opera was able to defray the expense of bringing marble from Carrara by offering some of it for sale as tombstones to the wealthier citizens of Florence. But at times marble tombstones originally destined to glorify deceased magistrates and wool merchants became part of the cupola instead. In July 1426, there was a shortage of good marble due to the high transport costs, causing the Opera to order the cutting up of tombstones – presumably those from a stockpile rather than ones already marking graves. But by that time it was clear that a cheaper and more expedient method of acquiring this precious stone was needed. And Filippo, ambitious and inventive as ever, had just the plan up his sleeve.

Water transport was considerably cheaper than overland carriage, which was prey to the vagaries of the terrain and the weather, the moods and endurance of the beasts of burden, and the frailty of the wagons. It was, for example, twelve times more expensive to transport grain by land to Florence than along the Arno.[1] But water transport to Florence was made difficult by the Arno's capricious flow, the volume and rate of which was highly variable, depending on the season and the weather. The fifty-mile stretch from Florence to Pisa was badly silted and, in the hot summer months, little more than a trickle. Unlike, say, the River Thames, the Arno had virtually no tide on which a vessel might ride. Galleys rowing to and from Pisa were sometimes forced to winch themselves forward with the help of trees along the river bank. In periods of heavy rain the Arno was even more impossible. During the *piena*, the spring flood, it became a frenzied torrent. Water hurtled down from the slopes of the Apennines, eroding its banks, smashing bridges and inundating both Florence and Pisa with monotonous regularity. Even under ideal conditions, flat-keeled barges could travel upriver only as far as the port of Signa, still ten miles from the gates of Florence, because of the shallow water and numerous sand banks. As a result, all cargo bound for Florence had to be transferred to mules or carts and padded with straw-filled sacks for the final stretch.

Various attempts were made to solve the problem of the Arno's fickle currents. Silt was scraped from its bed by dredgers – barges rigged with treadmills powering buckets or scoops fixed at the end of long shafts. But with each flood the silt returned. River banks pulverised by floodwaters were shored up with the wrecks of old galleys, but these were always liable to drift away again. In 1444, in one of his last acts as a civil engineer, Filippo would fortify the bank of the Arno near the Porto San Marco in Pisa. Decades later, and most ambitious of all, Leonardo da Vinci planned to bypass the clogged artery of the Arno altogether by constructing a 50-foot-wide canal that would leave the Arno near Florence and run through Prato and Pistoia, 25 miles to the northeast, before swinging south and rejoining the river at Vicopisano, a few miles upstream from Pisa. This venture, like most of Leonardo's plans, was never carried out.

But in 1426 Filippo had in mind a different solution to the problem of river transport. An innovator in countless other areas, he had also received, in 1421, the world's first ever patent for invention.[2] Describing the *capomaestro* as 'a man of the most perspicacious intellect, industry and invention', this document granted him a patent of monopoly for 'some machine or kind of ship, by means of which he thinks he can easily, at any time, bring in any merchandise and load on the river Arno and on any other river or water, for less money than usual'.[3] Until this point no patent system existed to prevent an inventor's designs from being stolen and copied by others. This is the reason why ciphers were so widely used by scientists and also why Filippo was so reluctant to share the secrets of his inventions with others. Filippo complained about this plagiarism to his friend Mariano Taccola in a bitter diatribe against the ignorant multitude:

> *Many are ready, when listening to the inventor, to belittle and deny his achievements, so that he will no longer be heard in honourable places. But after some months or a year they use the inventor's words, in speech or writing or design. They boldly call themselves the inventors of the things that they first condemned, and attribute the glory of another to themselves.*[4]

The patent for invention was designed to remedy this situation.

Possibly Filippo already had in mind a cheaper and more effective means of shipping marble up the Arno; but the patent makes clear that the invention would have a wide application, being of great benefit 'to merchants and others'. Once built, this curious-looking vessel quickly became known as *Il Badalone*, or 'the Monster'. According to the terms of the patent, any boat copying its design, and thereby violating Filippo's monopoly, would be condemned to flames.

Not much is known about the precise design of *Il Badalone*, the finer points of whose construction Filippo, despite the protection of his patent, kept secret for fear of imitators. Manetti and Vasari do not even mention the episode, which does not exactly redound to their hero's glory. However, it must have been technologically novel and adventurous in order to be deemed worthy of a patent. The nickname implies a great and perhaps even ungainly size, which would have been one of the boat's chief economic advantages – and possibly also the source of its undoing.

The only picture we have of the boat was done by Mariano Taccola, to whom the *capomaestro*, in a rare fit of candour, appears to have described its construction. In his book *De ingeneis* Taccola shows how a wagon with fourteen wheels that transports the marble overland from the quarry can be converted into a raft tugged by a rowing-boat. We know that in 1427 Filippo borrowed from the Opera a rope with which to tow *Il Badalone*. It is therefore very likely that the boat consisted of a large, raft-like wooden platform possibly buoyed by a number of floats, such as barrels, and tugged along the river either by another boat or by oxen toiling up the towpath. But even Taccola, a skilled engineer, appears to have been flummoxed by the design: he attempts a description of *Il Badalone* only to find that his pen fails him. 'Let it be known that one cannot explain each and every detail,' he writes in some frustration. 'Ingenuity resides in the mind and intelligence of the architect rather than in drawing and writing.'

Whatever the boat's design, its first and only known employment was the shipment of marble for the ribs of the dome. One year after the Opera had been forced to use tombstones in its building, Filippo acquired a

20. Taccola's version of *Il Badalone*.

contract to transport 100,000 pounds of white marble from Pisa. With his ingenious new boat he calculated that he would reduce the shipping cost by almost half, lowering it from 7 lire and 10 soldi per ton to 4 lire and 14 soldi.

Not everyone was so optimistic. *Il Badalone* appears to have been a source of ridicule from the start, a stick which Filippo's enemies, temporarily overawed by his astonishing success with the dome, now gleefully used to beat him. Most vocal of these was his old adversary Giovanni da Prato, who composed a sonnet attacking Filippo and his latest invention, which he described scathingly as an *acque vola*, or 'water bird'. This description implies that *Il Badalone*, rather like a Mississippi steamboat, may have featured paddle-wheels, the sight of which, thrashing in the water like an awkward pair of wings, could have inspired Giovanni's insulting nickname. Such paddle-wheels, powered by treadmills, were certainly at a design stage a few years later.

21. A sketch of a boat with paddle wheels by the Sienese inventor
Francesco di Giorgio.

Giovanni's ill-humoured piece of verse makes his earlier comments
regarding the faulty profile of the dome seem positively tame by
comparison. He not only mocks the famous *capomaestro* as a 'pit of
ignorance' and a 'miserable beast and imbecile', but furthermore promises
to commit suicide should Filippo's plan succeed. Filippo was not one to
suffer such discourtesies in silence. He may not have been a man of letters
of the same stature, but he was no stranger to literary pursuits, as his study
of Dante proves. He composed a sonnet of his own, equally caustic, in
which he derided his distinguished opponent as a 'ridiculous-looking
beast' who was incapable of understanding the mysteries of nature in his –
Filippo's – ingenious designs. These exchanges became so rancorous that a
short time later Filippo was among the citizens of Florence made to swear

an oath to 'forgive injuries, lay down all hatred, entirely free themselves of any faction and bias, and to attend only to the good and the honour and the greatness of the Republic, forgetting all offences received to this day through passions of party or faction or for any other reason'. It was an oath that, in the years to come, Filippo would find difficult to keep.

In the end, Giovanni da Prato was not required to carry out his grisly promise to kill himself. Problems taxed the enterprise from the start. Although the patent was granted in 1421, *Il Badalone* did not make her maiden voyage for another seven years, by which time the patent, originally for three years, had needed to be renewed at least once. In the summer of 1426 Filippo travelled to Pisa to confer with the Consul of Maritime Affairs regarding the heightening of the city's fortifications. It seems likely that he took the opportunity to negotiate over *Il Badalone*, for the Consul of Maritime Affairs inspected boats and merchandise passing through Pisa and issued permits for all crafts using the Arno. *Il Badalone* was possibly even built in Pisa, which had long been renowned for its shipwrights. The galleys of the new Florentine navy – the first of which had sailed for Alexandria in 1422 – were at that time under construction in its dockyards. In any case, one day in early May 1428 Filippo's revolutionary new boat, laden with 100 tons of white marble, was launched from the dock at Pisa, in the shadow of another, leaning, technological folly.

It is not clear whether disaster struck because of a design flaw, the Arno's treacherous sandbanks and currents, or some other mishap: the precise details of *Il Badalone's* fate have not been recorded. We do know that the boat not only failed to reach Florence, it did not even make Signa. It either sank or became stranded near Empoli, 25 miles from Pisa, with the loss of its entire load. Shortly thereafter anxious officials from the Opera notified Filippo that he was 'required within eight days ... to ship by small boats to the Opera that quantity of white marble which he had shipped on the *Badalone* from the city of Pisa to Empoli'.

The order was not executed within the time stipulated. Two months after the abortive journey Filippo was purchasing a 240-pound rope with which to salvage either the stricken vessel or her cargo – a humiliating spectacle that Giovanni da Prato must have contemplated with relish. How Filippo attempted to recover the load from the bed of the Arno is not known, but a sketch by Taccola shows two stone-laden barges being used to raise a sunken marble column. Such salvage operations exercised the ingenuity and imagination of a number of engineers during the fifteenth century, leading to several attempts to design diving suits. Both Taccola and Francesco di Giorgio invented various types of breathing apparatus and underwater mask, as well as inflatable bladders to raise and lower divers. These works bore fruit in 1446 when, in one of the most celebrated engineering feats of the century, Alberti raised part of the hull of one of Caligula's ships from the bottom of Lake Nemi by using divers from Genoa.

Filippo, however, met with no such success on the Arno. Almost four and a half years later the Opera was still pressing him to fulfil his contract to bring the errant 100 tons of marble to Florence – still, optimistically enough, on *Il Badalone*, which must have survived the wreck. In March 1433 Battista d'Antonio was forced to resort to the old and unsatisfactory expedient of cutting up tomb slabs for use on the dome. And that summer the Opera finally lost faith in Filippo and his wayward vessel, negotiating instead with three other contractors, who promised to deliver 600 tons of marble to Florence at a cost of 7 lire 10 soldi per ton – almost double Filippo's proposed price.

Filippo had built *Il Badalone* and contracted for the load of marble entirely out of his own pocket. Altogether he lost 1,000 florins on the venture – the equivalent of ten years of his salary as *capomaestro* and roughly one-third of his total wealth. It must have been a cruel blow for a man who had envisioned reaping lucrative financial rewards from his invention. Even worse, his reputation as the modern Archimedes was tarnished – a reputation that would be undermined still further a few years later, when another of his clever plans was to rebound disastrously.

Débâcle at Lucca

A FEW WEEKS BEFORE *Il Badalone* weighed anchor, Filippo had ridden on horseback into the nearby hills in order to oversee the extraction of yet more sandstone from the Trassinaia quarry. The dome had by this time reached a height of over 100 feet, meaning that the teams of masons were now working 270 feet above the ground, or the equivalent of 20 storeys in the air. As the shells curved ever inwards they began preparing to install the third of the sandstone chains. The beams started arriving in the Piazza del Duomo at the beginning of 1429. In preparation for laying them, Filippo's *castello* was refurbished with a new set of pulley wheels.

Despite the embarrassing catastrophe of *Il Badalone*, the Opera del Duomo still displayed confidence in Filippo's inventions and designs. The *rota magna*, the old treadmill built in 1396, was decommissioned and sold, having been rendered obsolete by the powerful new ox-hoist. Also sold was the timber used for the centring of the vaults in the tribunes. This latter act in particular revealed just how much faith Filippo inspired in the wardens. Deeply sceptical of his plans a decade earlier, they were now clearly convinced that the cupola could be raised without the use of a wooden centring. The evidence was, after all, right before their eyes in the shape of the half-finished dome. In fact, so confident had they become, that Neri di Fioravanti's 1367 model of the cathedral, once so sacred, now served the Opera as a lavatory.

Work on the third sandstone chain did not proceed quite as expected, however, and it would not be completed for another four years. The dome project was about to encounter its first serious delay. Construction first began to slow down when, in the summer of 1429, cracks were discovered in the side walls at the east end of the nave – that is, the end of the nave nearest the dome. Barely a year after the failure of *Il Badalone*, Filippo suddenly found himself faced with a potentially more serious disaster. It seemed that the church, as constructed, might simply be unable to support the heavy load of the dome.

There were no immediate signs of panic in the Opera del Duomo. Filippo was consulted by the wardens and, bold as ever, put forth one of his typically audacious proposals: he viewed the cracking walls as an opportunity to remodel the entire cathedral. What he now envisioned was a building different from the 1367 model but one that imitated another of Neri di Fioravanti's designs instead: that of Santa Trìnita, the Gothic church beside the Arno that had been reconstructed by Neri on the site of a much older structure. Following Neri's design, Filippo proposed to flank the side aisles of the cathedral with a series of chapels.

Filippo had already built or planned a number of such chapels in various of Florence's churches, including the Barbadori Chapel in Santa Felìcita and the Ridolfi Chapel in San Jacopo. And in 1428 he had begun rebuilding the Augustinian church of Santo Spirito, which he planned to encircle with no fewer than thirty-six chapels, each belonging to a different family. It was the tradition in Florence for the bones of the wealthy to reside in splendour in special chapels within the churches (while those of Florence's poor were piled in the charnel-house). The remains of the Medici family lie in San Lorenzo, the Pazzis' in Santa Croce. In fact, Florence's churches were so crammed with tombs that during the fifteenth century one bishop voiced concerns about so many corpses defiling the House of God. His worries might also have been justified on the grounds of public health: in times of plague it was always the houses nearest the churches that were the first to become infected.

The chapels that Filippo was proposing for Santa Maria del Fiore would do more than serve as repositories for the bodies of Florence's finest citizens: they would form what he called a *catena totius ecclesie*, or a 'chain around the church'. Like the flying buttresses on the sides of Gothic cathedrals, they were to serve as abutments, bracing the walls of the nave against the outward thrust caused by the weight of the dome. Filippo assured the wardens that Santa Maria del Fiore would also be made much more beautiful as a result.

In September 1429 Filippo was ordered to begin work on a model. The wardens were interested not only in how the chapels might stabilise the cathedral but also how they could be incorporated into its existing structure, the external walls of which were already encrusted with marble and decorated with sculpture. Would all of this painstaking artistry have to be refurbished or removed? And at what expense to the Wool Guild? Work had barely begun on this new model, however, when another distraction arose. In November 1429 Florentine mercenaries attacked Lucca, the wool- and silk-weaving city 40 miles to the west. It was to be an unexpectedly long and damaging campaign.

For so long prey to both plagues and wars, Florence had enjoyed a brief respite for the first few years of the dome's construction. A war with the Kingdom of Naples had ended in 1414 when, in one of those miraculous events to which the Florentines were becoming accustomed, an earthquake shattered Naples and the enemy warlord King Ladislaus died of a fever. For the next ten years Florence experienced a period of peace, but then in the summer of 1424 Florence went to war once again. This time the enemy was the new Duke of Milan, Filippo Maria Visconti.

Filippo Maria was as formidable a foe as his late father, that ruthless enemy of Florence, Giangaleazzo. And he was demented even by the standards of the Visconti family. Terrified of thunder, he would cower in a sound-proof room during storms, while in better weather he enjoyed rolling naked in the grass. Gluttonous and obese, he was unable to mount a horse or even walk unaided, and so sensitive was he about his ugliness that he refused to have his portrait painted. His second wife was imprisoned after the duke, a superstitious man, heard a dog howl on their wedding night. Her fate was preferable, however, to that of his first bride, who had been beheaded.

Filippo Maria picked up where his late father had left off: in 1422 his troops captured both Brescia and Genoa, and a year later they seized the town of Forlì, only 50 miles from Florence. The following year, as plague raged through Tuscany, his forces defeated the Florentines at Zagonara, in Romagna. There were only three casualties, all Florentine soldiers who fell from their horses and drowned on the battlefield in their heavy plate-armour (it had rained heavily in Zagonara the night before). This lack of bloodshed shows that warfare in the Middle Ages and Renaissance, contrary to popular conceptions, could be reasonably civilised. Most battles resembled chess matches in which opposing commanders sought to outmanoeuvre each other, the loser being the one who conceded that his position was technically vulnerable. These engagements were fought by mercenaries who settled the terms of warfare in advance, rather like sportsmen deciding the rules of a game. As a notary for the Commune, Filippo's father had frequently been involved in these negotiations, travelling far afield to engage the services of mercenaries such as the Englishman Sir John Hawkwood, who had commanded the Florentine army between 1377 and 1394. By common agreement the armies declined to fight in certain conditions: at night, in winter, on steep slopes or on boggy ground. The engagements were not always quite so congenial, however: six months after Zagonara the Florentines lost an entire army against the Milanese at Valdilamone.

The battles against Lucca were even more disastrous. A truce had been signed with Filippo Maria in April 1428, when, to celebrate the occasion, torches were burned on the walls of Santa Maria del Fiore. But the ink was barely dry on the treaty when the Florentines set their sights on their neighbour. Like many medieval cities, Lucca had suffered a chequered past, passing from the hands of one warring state to another. In the previous hundred years it had been occupied by the Bavarians, sold to the Genoese, seized by the King of Bohemia, pawned to Parma, ceded to Verona, and finally sold to Florence. Now war was advanced by the Florentines on the pretext that Lucca's ruler, Paolo Guinigi, had secretly been supporting the Duke of Milan. The campaign went badly from the outset, with the Republic soon getting bogged down in an unsuccessful war against a smaller and weaker foe. After several months of stalemate the Dieci della Balìa (the War Office) decided to unleash their secret weapon: in March 1430 Filippo Brunelleschi was sent into the field.

It was by no means unusual for an architect to become involved in a military campaign during the Middle Ages. Besides the cathedral in Florence, the Opera del Duomo was responsible for all military architecture within the Florentine domains. The men who built Santa Maria del Fiore were therefore the same ones who fortified Florence and its neighbours with walls, moats and bastions. Some ten years before starting work on the foundations of the new cathedral, Arnolfo di Cambio began raising a set of defensive walls around Florence. These massive fortifications were completed by Giotto in the 1330s. Two centuries later Michelangelo would rebuild these walls, raising bastions around San Miniato with unbaked bricks made from hemp and dung. And Leonardo da Vinci was forever drawing plans for weapons of war, including scythed chariots, steam cannons and gigantic crossbows.

Like Arnolfo di Cambio and Giotto, Filippo was expected to carry out military commissions as a regular part of his duties. It was a busy time to hold the post of *capomaestro*, for during the 1420s towns throughout Tuscany were being buttressed as protection against the mortars and siege engines of the Milanese. Filippo was involved in fortifying Pistoia as early as 1423, and a year later he began work at Malmantile, a stronghold in the Arno valley between Florence and Pisa. This fortress was completed two years later, when parapets, battlements, towers and a moat were in place.

Unlike many of Filippo's other architectural commissions, this stronghold was of a fairly traditional design. It operated on the time-honoured principle that any assailants who survived the hail of arrows and crossbows fired from the walls, and then managed to cross the moat, would be crushed to death by large stones dropped from the parapets.

These were all defensive manoeuvres, however. What was required in 1430 was an offensive weapon – some means of subduing the stubborn Lucchese once and for all. Mortars were being fired at Lucca from a distance of 1,200 feet, and the city's walls had been badly damaged. But still the Lucchese failed to relent.

The technology of warfare was undergoing a transition during the fifteenth century. Gunpowder – seen by many as a devilish invention – had been introduced in the previous century, and large-calibre cannons were being cast, along with projectiles weighing several hundred pounds. However, since the formula for gunpowder (a mixture of saltpetre, sulphur and charcoal) had yet to be perfected, ancient and medieval devices such as siege engines, catapults and battering-rams were still in widespread use. Plans for both sorts of weapons are shown in a manuscript from the 1430s, *De machinis*, written by Filippo's friend Mariano Taccola. This treatise includes diagrams and descriptions of traditional devices such as articulated siege ladders and a bewildering array of catapults for hurling boulders at the enemy. There are also bombards and barrels filled with gunpowder and equipped with fuses. One of Taccola's most celebrated designs involved exploding a keg of gunpowder in a tunnel excavated under an enemy stronghold (a ploy that would re-emerge at the Battle of the Somme in 1916). No direct evidence exists of Filippo's collaboration on these designs, but scholars have speculated that the *capomaestro* may have originated at least some of them.[1] Certainly a number of the catapults – loaded by hoists and powered by counterweights – were well within Filippo's widely recognised area of expertise. However, his plans for subduing Lucca involved something much more ambitious.

Lucca had been the first city in Tuscany to adopt Christianity. According to legend it had been converted by St Frediano, an Irish monk who saved the city from flooding by diverting the dangerously swollen River Serchio. Perhaps inspired by this legend, Filippo proposed to reverse the saint's miracle by altering the course of the Serchio and stranding Lucca in the middle of a lake contained by a dam. Cut off from the countryside, the Lucchese would have little recourse but to surrender.

Filippo's plan was not an original one. Hydraulic engineering was used in warfare even in ancient times. In 510 BC, for instance, Milo, the ruler of Croton and patron of Pythagoras, diverted the River Crathis and flooded the warring town of Sybaris, an ancient city in southern Italy which archaologists have only recently uncovered. Some two hundred years later Sostratus of Cnidus captured Memphis for Ptolemy I, the King of Egypt, by changing the course of the Nile and dividing the town in two. More recently a Florentine engineer named Domenico di Benintendi had constructed for Giangaleazzo Visconti a number of gigantic dykes with which the duke hoped to redirect the River Mincio and flood the city of Mantua under 20 feet of water. The plan was never put into effect, though the remains of one of these dykes may still be seen at Valeggio. Fortunately, the duke was also unable to carry through another of his ambitious plans: to drain the canals of Venice, thereby rendering the Venetians defenceless.

Filippo appears to have acquired some expertise in hydraulic engineering a short time before the Lucca project. During the late 1420s he travelled to Siena to consult with Taccola, whose speciality it was. Hydraulics enjoyed a long tradition in Siena, where the shortage of water had been remedied by the construction during the Middle Ages of the *bottini*, 16 miles of underground tunnels, complete with filters and settling tanks, that conveyed fresh water to the city. During Taccola's time this supply of water was being increased and numerous fountains built. Taccola's *De ingeneis* showed how to build dams, bridges, flood controls, underwater foundations, aqueducts and various other waterworks. As we have seen, this treatise also depicted and attempted to describe *Il Badalone*.

In a manuscript discovered at the end of the nineteenth century, Taccola records a conversation with Filippo that took place during this visit to Siena. Although Filippo is not known to have had any practical experience of hydraulic engineering before the Lucca project, he nevertheless speaks with some authority on the subject, exchanging ideas with Taccola on the best means of building dams and bridges. Special attention was given to sinking their foundations. Filippo warned Taccola that if the river bed consisted of large pieces of tufa – the lightweight, porous rock that the *capomaestro* had considered using in the upper part of the dome – it was better not to drive piles, since they would break the tufa and cause the water to flow through, carrying away the dam or bridge. These words of caution turned out to be lamentably ironic. Despite Filippo's theoretical preparations for the project, his enormous dam was a failure. Indeed, the Lucca disaster would be much more harmful to Filippo's reputation than the wreck of *Il Badalone*.

Work on the project proceeded slowly due to a lack of funds. Then doubts were raised about the strength of the dam even before it was completed. In May 1430 the notary in the Florentine camp outside Lucca wrote to the War Office that after studying Filippo's design he remained unconvinced that the dam could withstand the weight of the water. But his arguments were skilfully parried by the *capomaestro*: 'To everything Pippo replies with arguments I cannot contradict,' wrote the flustered notary, 'though I do not know if this is because I do not know more of this matter. Soon we shall see what will come of all of this.'

Others in the Florentine camp were even more pessimistic about the project. Rather than arguing with Filippo, as the notary had done, Neri Capponi, the commissioner for the Florentine army, simply sent his men to inspect the dam and make up their own minds about its robustness. Apparently one did not need to be an expert in hydraulics in order to realise that Filippo's plan was ripe for miscarriage.

Filippo ignored these warnings, evidently unchastened by his humiliating disaster with *Il Badalone*, whose cargo, these two years later, he was still attempting to recover. His stubbornness on the issue was the result of his usual contempt for his critics. After all, had not his designs for the dome been mocked in the same way? And was not the dome, by all accounts, a great success? In his conversation with Taccola he had condemned the *capocchis et ignorantibus* ('blockheads and ignoramuses') who could not understand the schemes of inventors like himself:

> *Every person wishes to know of the proposals, the learned and the ignorant. The learned understands the work proposed — he understands at least something, partly or fully — but the ignorant and inexperienced understand nothing, not even when things are explained to them. Their ignorance moves them promptly to anger. They remain in ignorance because they want to show themselves learned, which they are not, and they move the other ignorant crowd to insistence on its own poor ways and to scorn for those who know.*[2]

The only thing to be done with such idiots, he claimed, was to march them off to war. These remarks were recorded before the Lucca enterprise: after the débâcle his plans for his critics may have been even less charitable.

Like the Florentines, the Lucchese must have realised that Filippo's project was far from foolproof. Initially they countered the attempt to flood the plain by building dams of their own, raising a number of high embankments that prevented the water from flowing in the planned direction. But the Lucchese were not content with these defensive manoeuvres, and so one night, in a brilliant military sortie, one of their garrisons sneaked into Florentine territory and breached the canal that Filippo had dug at its point of deviation from the Serchio. The plain around Lucca was flooded, just as Filippo had predicted. However, the result was (as Machiavelli would sardonically remark in his history of Florence) 'contrary to his expectations': with devastating force the waters of the river swept away the dam and, worse still, flooded the Florentine camp. Instead of attacking Lucca, as planned, the Florentines were forced to beat a hasty retreat on to higher ground. Besides his reputation as an engineer, Filippo left behind something else on the swamped field outside Lucca: the tax reports for 1431 reveal that he lost his bed, which had been kept in his tent in the Florentine camp.

The war went from bad to worse. Eager to weaken Florence, the Duke of Milan dispatched troops to Lucca. The Florentines countered by bribing the duke's military commander, Count Sforza, to quit the city. Sforza duly departed from Lucca, but in the battle that followed, the Florentines were soundly defeated. Morale ebbed swiftly away.

Filippo was not alone in being blamed for the defeat. A familiar scapegoat was used to explain the Florentines' ineptness in battle: homosexuality. For years clergymen such as the Franciscan firebrand Bernardino of Siena had been raging from the pulpit that the crime of sodomy was destroying the city. So famous was Florence for homosexual activity that during the fourteenth century the German slang for 'sodomite' was *Florenzer*. In 1432 the government took steps to curtail this perceived root of its troubles on the battlefield by establishing an agency to identify and prosecute homosexuals, the Ufficiali di Notte, or 'Office of the Night' (a name made even more colourful by the fact that *notte* was slang for 'bugger'). This vice squad worked in tandem with the Orwellian-sounding Ufficiali dell'Onestà, or the 'Office of Decency', which was charged with licensing and administering the municipal brothels that had been created in the area around the Mercato Vecchio.* The specific aim of these public brothels was to wean Florentine men from the 'greater evil' of sodomy. Prostitutes became a common sight in Florence, not least because the law required them to wear a distinctive garb: gloves, high-heeled shoes and a bell on the head.

Despite these measures the Florentines fared little better on the battlefield. The Duke of Milan persuaded Genoa, Siena and Piombino to enter into a league against the battered Republic. Seeing the writing on the wall, the Florentines sued for peace, and a truce was finally signed in 1433, though hostilities with Milan would not really end until the duke's death over a decade later.

---

* A less official method of detecting homosexuals was for mothers to rattle their sons' coin bags: if the coins exclaimed 'fire, fire, fire' the money was said to be the gift of a sodomite.

From Bad to Worse

THE WAR AGAINST Lucca took a severe toll on the building site at Santa Maria del Fiore. As the campaign began, the wages of most of the masons were halved, with some salaries falling much more drastically, from 1 lira per day to a positively stingy 1 lira per month. Even Filippo himself faced a pay cut: his salary dropped from 100 florins per year to 50. Then in December 1430 over forty masons on the building site and in the quarries at Trassinaia were made redundant, partly because of the cold weather but also in order to save money. Construction throughout Florence had ground to a halt as funds intended for various buildings (including the oratory of Santa Maria degli Angeli, another of Filippo's projects) were diverted to the war effort. As commissions dried up, many artists, including Donatello, left Florence for more peaceful, prosperous cities.

Given this belt-tightening regime, Filippo had selected a truly unfavourable moment to press his expensive plan to remodel the cathedral with a ring of chapels. Predictably his model met with little enthusiasm among the wardens, who decided to go for a cheaper option and reinforce the nave of the church with visible iron tie rods. Filippo accepted their decision, but only grudgingly. At the beginning of 1431 he designed a model for these rods and subsequently won the commission to install them. Within a month of this commission a significant decision was taken by the wardens: they ordered that Neri di Fioravanti's 1367 model should be destroyed. The cupola, they reasoned, was now 'beyond all comparison' with Neri's model. This was not to say that Filippo had violated the model, but that, with the structure so close to completion, Neri's model had lost its function as a touchstone and building could continue without any further reference to it.

In the end, both iron and wooden ties were used to prevent further cracks in the nave. Owing to his lack of enthusiasm for this solution, Filippo proceeded at a fairly leisurely pace in their installation, and in May 1433 the wardens had to order him to hurry up. A year later, after the work was completed, he complained about their ugliness in a submission to the Opera. He believed that if his proposed chapels were built these eyesores could be removed, and so once again he began pressing the wardens to reconsider his plan. Although they allowed him to complete his abandoned model, their final answer was categorical: he was to forget his ring of chapels and concentrate instead on completing the dome. The wardens, understandably, were impatient to see the structure finished. They had been hoping to hold services under the cupola in 1433, but this timetable had been grossly optimistic and eighteen months later, when they came together to discuss Filippo's model for the chapels, the date of completion seemed no nearer.

This episode marks one of the few times that Filippo was unable to win over the wardens to his point of view. But his annoyance must have been eclipsed by other, more pressing worries, for in August 1434, just a few days after the meeting of the wardens and Wool consuls, he was arrested and thrown into prison. His crime: failing to pay his annual dues to the Masons Guild. His life seemed to be going from bad to worse.

The Arte dei Maestri di Pietra e di Legname, the 'Guild of Stonemasons and Carpenters', was one of the largest of the Florentine guilds. It was run, like the other guilds, not so much for the benefit of its members – the common labourers and stonemasons – as for the political elite of the city.

The guilds were the nominal foundation of the Republican constitution, because membership in one of them was a qualification for any political office. But power had actually come to be concentrated in the guild court of the Mercanzia, which had been founded in 1309 and was controlled by a network of wealthy, intermarrying and often rival families, including the Capponi, the Medici, the Strozzi, the Bardi and the Spini. Through the Mercanzia this economic elite extended its power into the running of the other guilds, controlling the selection of candidates eligible for guild office.

In the Middle Ages the Masons Guilds of northern Europe had become the jealous guardians of the 'mysteries' of their profession. In a famous case from 1099, for example, the Bishop of Utrecht was murdered by a master mason whose son he had persuaded to reveal the secret of laying out the foundation of a church. There were, of course, obvious reasons for maintaining a monopoly on this sort of information: the masons had an economic interest in not disseminating their knowledge beyond the guild.

In Florence, however, the Masons Guild was never so obsessively jealous of its secrets. It was possible not only for carpenters and masons from outside Florence to practise their craft within the city but also for craftsmen from other guilds to work in the building trade. The guild did not seem anxious to require membership of such men, much less dues. Neither Giotto nor Andrea Pisano, two previous *capomaestri*, ever joined it. Filippo had even been granted an exemption that permitted him to work as an architect without having matriculated in the guild, a fact that made the sudden demand for membership dues – and his arrest – all the more bizarre.

Filippo's arrest is certainly suspicious. The dues for one year would have amounted to the grand total of 12 soldi, or roughly the amount that a common labourer on the site of Santa Maria del Fiore could earn in a single day of work. Surviving records show that, despite this modest rate, the accounts of many members of the guild were in arrears.[1] But only Filippo was ever arrested and imprisoned for nonpayment. Clearly sinister forces were at work to ruin the *capomaestro*.

Filippo had been politically active in Florence throughout the course of his work on the dome, serving numerous times on the councils that passed and rejected legislation proposed by the *Signoria*.[2] But he was rapidly falling out of favour with the Florentine ruling class. What was more, his wealthy patron Cosimo de' Medici — the man whose family had commissioned him to rebuild the church of San Lorenzo in 1425 — was now in exile. Cosimo's departure was a blow to the artists of Florence. After the death of his father, Giovanni, in 1429, he had become head of the powerful Medici bank. A learned man, Cosimo read Greek philosophy, collected ancient manuscripts and coins, befriended the humanist scholars and, following the example of the ancient Romans, rose early each morning in order to tend to his orchards and vineyards. His political career was a little less idyllic, however. He had been one of the members of the War Office who prosecuted the unsuccessful campaign against Lucca and in the wake of this failure he was arrested on a trumped-up charge of plotting to overthrow the government. In September 1433 he was imprisoned in the tower of the Palazzo della Signoria and shortly afterwards banished to Venice.

Like Cosimo, Filippo was in a weakened state following the disaster on the battlefield at Lucca. His reputation had been damaged, his most powerful patron was in exile and his work on the dome — though proceeding successfully — had been slowed due to a shortage of both manpower and funds. It was at this moment, therefore, that his enemies chose to pounce. The man behind his imprisonment was Raynaldo Silvestri, one of the consuls of the Masons Guild. It is tempting to ask if Silvestri was acting for anyone else besides the guild consuls. What, for example, might have been the role of Lorenzo Ghiberti or Giovanni da Prato? Lorenzo was immune from arrest on a similar charge, for he had joined the Masons Guild eight years earlier after having worked in the profession for almost a decade while still a member of the Silk Guild, to which Filippo also belonged. Late in life he would become a pillar of his new guild, serving as a consul between 1449 and 1453. But no evidence exists to suggest that the arrest was an intrigue on his part. It is more likely that it was instigated at the behest of the same people – the powerful Albizzi faction – who had engineered the exile of Cosimo de' Medici.

All things considered, Filippo's incarceration could have been much worse than it was. He was not held like a common criminal in Florence's communal prison, the Stinche, nor in the artificial underground caves, the *burelle*, that served as Florence's dungeons. The populations of these prisons consisted mainly of paupers unable to pay fines levied against them, as well as forgers, adulterers, thieves and gamblers. It was to this former prison, which stood near the Piazza Santa Croce, that Manetto, the Fat Carpenter, had been brought as part of Filippo's scheme against him. Also held in the Stinche were more serious criminals – heretics, sorcerers, witches and murderers – for whom unpleasant fates awaited: decapitation, amputation or burning at the stake. Executions took place outside the walls, in the Prato della Giustizia, the 'Field of Justice'. These were popular public spectacles – so popular, in fact, that criminals often had to be imported from other cities to satisfy the public's demand for macabre drama.

Filippo enjoyed a somewhat happier time. He was confined inside the prison of the Mercanzia, which was located in the Piazza della Signoria, and soon after his imprisonment the wardens of the Opera came to his rescue. Furious at his treatment, they insisted that the Capitano del Popolo, Florence's chief of police, arrest Raynaldo Silvestri. Filippo was released from prison a few days later, on 31 August, having spent the better part of two weeks in confinement. On the following day a pro-Medici government was elected, Cosimo recalled from Venice and Rinaldo Albizzi – leader of the rival faction – sent into exile. But if Filippo thought that his problems were over and he could now concentrate his efforts solely on the cupola, he was sadly mistaken. Less than two months later, in October, his adopted son, Buggiano, stole money and jewels from his house and fled to Naples.

Andrea Cavalcanti, or 'Il Buggiano', had lived with Filippo for fifteen years, ever since he was brought to Florence at the age of seven. Filippo probably first met the boy in the Tuscan village of Buggiano, near Pistoia, where Ser Brunellesco, his father, had owned a plot of land with vines and olive trees. In 1434, Buggiano was already making his mark in Florence as a sculptor. Filippo had employed him on a number of prestigious projects, including the cathedral, for which he sculpted a marble lavabo, the ritual hand-basin in the south sacristy. Nearby in San Lorenzo he had worked on an even more prominent commission: the sarcophagus for Giovanni de' Medici and his wife Piccarda, the parents of Cosimo de' Medici.

Little is known of Buggiano's early life, but his education and upbringing must have been similar to Filippo's, and he became a master in the Silk Guild at twenty-one. It was natural for a son in Florence to apprentice in his father's workshop. Lorenzo Ghiberti, who worked at the foundry of his stepfather Bartoluccio, would later be succeeded by his own two sons and then by his grandson Buonaccorso. Similarly, the *capomaestro* Battista d'Antonio was assisted in his work on the cupola by his son Antonio. In fact, Antonio would even be named as a *capomaestro*. What is odd about this latter arrangement — apart from the fact that yet another *capomaestro* was deemed necessary — is the fact that in 1430, the year of his appointment, Antonio di Battista was only eleven years old. At this tender age he was not even old enough to be apprenticed to a stonemason, let alone be put in charge of the century's grandest building project. Strange as it may seem, such an arrangement was not unprecedented. Minors were sometimes named as heads of industrial firms in Florence even though they had no actual input in the running of the business. In 1402 Cosimo de' Medici, then thirteen, was named head of the Medici's wool-manufacturing firm. Not surprisingly, the actual administration was left to an experienced manager. Similarly, the participation on the cupola project of Antonio di Battista, the boy-*capomaestro*, seems to have been minimal and his position only nominal.

Buggiano's position, whether at the cathedral or in San Lorenzo, was far from nominal. By executing commissions such as the sarcophagus for Giovanni de' Medici he freed Filippo to work on his designs and models for the cupola and also to seek out further work. Buggiano was, moreover, a very skilled sculptor: at times his work is indistinguishable from that of Filippo, and at other times he even surpasses his master.[3] Filippo cannot have been an easy person to work for, given his volatile, demanding and stubborn nature. And, for whatever reason, he seems to have treated the young man rather casually. He failed, for example, to pay him the substantial sum of 200 florins – two years' worth of wages – for his work on the cathedral and in San Lorenzo. Buggiano therefore took the money and jewels as his remuneration and absconded to Naples, where he presumably planned to make his way in the world without the assistance of the *capomaestro*.

Filippo should not have experienced any difficulties meeting this payment given the fact that in 1433, despite his losses over *Il Badalone*, he was still worth the considerable sum of 5,000 florins. But the *capomaestro*, a genius in so many other areas, was not as skilled as he might have been at handling his finances. This tendency was not unusual, since a carefree attitude towards money was typical of many of Florence's great artists and sculptors. Filippo's friend Masaccio would make loans without bothering to collect them, and Donatello was said to have left sitting on his worktable a basket of money from which his apprentices were free to help themselves. Filippo could be equally generous, giving much of his money to the poor, but his casual attitude to his finances was sometimes not so much charitable as negligent. In September 1418, for example, his political career had suffered a temporary setback when tax arrears rendered him ineligible for office. His timing in that case could hardly have been worse given that the cupola competition had been announced only a month earlier.

Buggiano was twenty-two when he absconded to Naples with Filippo's possessions. Although already a master carver, he was still deemed an adolescent by Florentine law. In fact, like all adolescents, he would not be emancipated from his father's authority until the age of twenty-four, and some of these 'adolescents' could even remain under the control of their fathers until they were twenty-eight. Little wonder that many of them chafed under this system: the fourteenth-century poet and storyteller

Franco Sacchetti wrote that five out of six sons wanted their father to die prematurely so they could be set free. And it is in this role, that of the father betrayed by an ungrateful son, that we now catch a glimpse of Filippo.

The full details of this unflattering incident remain obscure because neither Vasari nor Manetti mentions it, just as they mention neither *Il Badalone* or the failed scheme to flood Lucca. Whatever the situation, Filippo was determined to have both Buggiano and his property returned. Unlike his friend Donatello, who had pursued one of his runaway apprentices to Ferrara, bent on murder, he proceeded along strictly legal lines, appealing to the highest authority: none other than Pope Eugenius IV. The young man's theft and flight therefore turned into an international incident.

Pope Eugenius had arrived in Florence in June, after being driven from the Lateran Palace by a stone-throwing mob of Romans made miserable and desperate from incessant warfare against the Duke of Milan, who was now harrying the Papal States. Eugenius had made his escape down the Tiber in disguise, sailed from Ostia, then disembarked at Livorno after a perilous journey. Altogether he would spend several years in Florence, where he would take part in a number of historic ceremonies in Santa Maria del Fiore.

The Papal Abbreviator at this time was Leon Battista Alberti, who had accompanied Eugenius to Florence. In 1434 Alberti was writing *De Pictura* ('On Painting'), the Italian version of which he would dedicate to Filippo two years later, with its praise of the amazing feat of 'Pippo the architect' in raising the dome. As Abbreviator, Alberti had the task of composing all of Eugenius's letters and bulls in impeccable and elegant Latin. Normally these bulls concerned doctrinal and liturgical matters, but on the twenty-third of October Alberti found himself promulgating what must have seemed a rather irregular edict: a request that Queen Giovanna of Naples immediately send Buggiano back to Florence along with the money and jewels taken from Filippo's house. A request from such a source could not be taken lightly, and the runaway sculptor was promptly returned to

Florence and the custody of his master. The embarrassing episode was thereby brought to a conclusion. Buggiano went back to work in Filippo's studio, dutifully executing further commissions for his master. No further such disputes appear to have arisen between the two men, and soon afterwards Buggiano was named as Filippo's heir.

Consecration

RELIGIOUS FEASTS WERE numerous in Florence, averaging almost one per week. The populace was accustomed to grand spectacles on these occasions: to the sight of priests and monks in rich habits of gold and silk bearing through the streets the standards of their orders and their most prized relics, all to the tolling of bells, the blaring of trumpets, the chanting of songs and the splashing of holy water. But in 1436 the Feast of the Annunciation, observed on the twenty-fifth of March, was the occasion for a celebration that was spectacular even by the standards of Florence.

On this day Pope Eugenius IV processed eastwards to the centre of the city from his residence in Santa Maria Novella. He was accompanied by seven cardinals, thirty-seven bishops and nine members of the Florentine government, including Cosimo de' Medici. The procession moved along a 1,000-foot-long wooden platform, six feet in height, that was bedecked with sweet-smelling flowers and herbs. This gangway had been designed by Filippo to carry the Pope safely above the crowds teeming in the streets below, a method of crowd control evidently selected in place of a much-used alternative, that of throwing coins into the street in order to scatter the people and keep them from pressing too closely upon the Holy Father. As the entourage turned into the Via de' Cerretani and creaked across the boardwalk in the direction of the thronging Piazza San Giovanni, the new cathedral rose suddenly into view. After 140 years of construction, the time had finally come to consecrate Santa Maria del Fiore.

Annunciation Day was an appropriate occasion for such a ceremony. The feast celebrates the appearance of the Archangel Gabriel before the Virgin Mary. In most depictions of the Annunciation, Gabriel is portrayed holding a lily, the symbol not only of purity but also of the city of Florence. He delivers to the Virgin tidings of the miracle to come: the intrusion of the divine into the realm of the human. For the people of Florence in 1436 the new cathedral must likewise have seemed a feat of divine intervention – though in this case the miracle had been performed not by an angel but by a man.

Santa Maria del Fiore had been carefully prepared for the ceremony. The makeshift wall dividing the octagon from the nave – a hoarding that separated the worshippers from the labourers – had finally been removed. A temporary wooden choir was erected according to Filippo's design and its twelve wooden statues of the Apostles given coats of paint. Linen curtains were fitted into the enormous windows of the drum in order to keep out the wind. Most noticeable of all, after fifteen years of almost continuous service the ox-hoist and its platform no longer stood in the middle of the octagon, which had now been paved with brick.

As the ceremony began, a cardinal proceeded along the new choir, moving from one of Filippo's wooden Apostles to another, lighting a candle in front of each. Eugenius climbed the steps of the altar, which was the cue for the chorus to begin singing its motet:

Lately the blossoms of roses, a gift from the Pope,
Despite the cruel cold of winter
Adorned the great edifice of the cathedral
Dedicated in perpetuity to thee,
Virgin of Heaven, holy and sanctified …

Eugenius meanwhile began placing all of the cathedral's relics on to the altar. Chief among these were the finger bone of St John the Baptist and the remains of the patron saint of Santa Maria del Fiore, Saint Zenobius, whose skull had been discovered in 1331 and placed inside a silver reliquary shaped like the dead saint's head.* As he did so, the cardinal began christening the red crosses in the hands each of the twelve wooden Apostles. By this act the cathedral was filled with the living presences of these saints, who were now capable, the Florentines believed, of working further miracles.

Though work had proceeded swiftly in the two years since Filippo's release from prison, the dome itself was not actually complete. In 1434 its walls had reached the required height of just over 144 *braccia*, or some 280 feet above the ground. A year later the masons had laid the fourth and final stone chain, which served as the closing ring at the top of the dome. But there was still much to be done. The exterior surface of the dome had yet to be tiled with terracotta, a task that would require another two years, and the facings of coloured marble would take more than another generation to complete. And the marble *lanterna*, or lantern (so called because of its appearance), had to be designed and then erected on top of the dome.

In 1436, however, the time seemed ripe for celebration. Therefore, on 30 August, five months after Pope Eugenius had consecrated the cathedral, the cupola itself was consecrated – a full sixteen years and two weeks after construction had begun. This ceremony was performed at nine o'clock in the morning by the Bishop of Fiesole, who climbed to the top of the dome to lay the final stone. Trumpets and fifes were played, church bells rang and the rooftops of the surrounding buildings were crowded with onlookers. Afterwards the *capomaestri* and the wardens descended from the cupola and indulged themselves with a meal of bread, wine, meat, fruit,

---

* An even more prized relic had so far eluded the Florentines: the skull of St John the Baptist. In 1411 the Commune had negotiated to purchase it from the Antipope John XXIII. The deal fell through, however, so some thirty years later the architect Filarete, acting as an agent for the Commune, tried to steal the skull and smuggle it to Florence. Caught in the act, he was sent to prison.

cheese and macaroni. The bulk of the enormous task lay behind them. The people of Florence had at last been given the dome they had dreamt of for almost seventy years, and Filippo had succeeded in performing an engineering feat whose structural daring was without parallel. Against enormous odds, he had achieved all that he had hoped to achieve ever since, as a boy, he had walked past the domeless cathedral and watched the groaning treadwheels at work. Seeing the new dome soaring over the city he must have been overwhelmed by the feeling that he had equalled, and even surpassed, the Romans whose works he had studied and admired. More than that, he must have felt that everything he had been made to suffer for the past two decades – the ridicule, the rivalries, the intrigues of his enemies – had been swept away by the scale of his accomplishment.

The Lantern

MOST DOMES FROM the Renaissance onwards feature lanterns at their summits. These usually serve a practical as well as a decorative purpose, admitting light into the interior of the dome as well as promoting ventilation. Neri di Fioravanti's model had included such a feature, as did Filippo's 1418 version, but with both of these models demolished – Filippo's one year after Neri's – no definitive design for a lantern existed.

Filippo must have felt by this point that the Opera del Duomo should automatically select him to design the lantern. But typically they announced another competition. In the summer of 1436 Filippo therefore began work on a model, as did Lorenzo Ghiberti and three other hopefuls. One can imagine Filippo's resentment: he would have been all too aware of the fact that, when Lorenzo finished the Baptistery doors in 1424, he was immediately commissioned to cast a further set – the 'Doors of Paradise' – without having to endure another competition. For Filippo the insult was no doubt worsened by the fact that one of his competitors for the design of the lantern was a lowly leadbeater. Another, worse still, was a woman.

The size and form of the lantern had been under discussion for several years. They would depend in part on the base on which its substructure was imposed – the sandstone chain at the top of the dome. Not installed until 1435, this chain had been the subject of considerable deliberation. As early as June 1432 a wooden model had been ordered by the Opera in order to determine its size and whether it should be octagonal like the first sandstone chain or circular like the arch-rings. Two months later the model was studied by the wardens, who selected an octagonal design but decided to reduce the diameter of the chain from 12 *braccia* to 10, or roughly 19 feet. A year later the diameter was again reduced slightly, this time to just under 10 *braccia*. Giovanni da Prato cannot have been pleased with these shrinking dimensions, for now even less light would be admitted into the church.

Filippo began constructing his model of the lantern with the help of a 31-year-old carpenter named Antonio di Ciaccheri Manetti. Antonio (not to be confused with Antonio di Tuccio Manetti, Filippo's biographer) was well known to the *capomaestro*. He had assisted Filippo with the wooden model of the closing ring, as well as with Filippo's design for the choir. The *capomaestro* would draw sketches of the lantern and send them to Antonio's workshop near the cathedral. Very soon, however, he had reason to regret his choice of collaborator. According to the biographer Manetti, Filippo was a better architect than a judge of character, for Antonio betrayed him by constructing a model of his own in which he unscrupulously incorporated many features of Filippo's design. This was exactly the sort of plagiarism the *capomaestro* had feared since the beginning of his career. But there was nothing to be done: Antonio's model was submitted to the Opera along with his own, Lorenzo Ghiberti's, and two others.

On the last day of 1436 the wardens met to examine the five models. Perhaps aware that their decision could prove controversial, they consulted widely: masters of theology, doctors of science, masons, goldsmiths, painters and a mathematician, as well as various influential citizens, including Cosimo de' Medici himself – all were called upon to offer their opinions. Their judgement, in the end, found in favour of Filippo's design, stating that his model would make for a stronger, better lit and more waterproof lantern. The wardens did, however, attach an important clause to their ruling, commanding Filippo to 'put aside all rancour remaining in him' (obviously they knew him well) and accept a number of suggested modifications to his design, however insignificant they might seem. The reason for this qualification was that Antonio had appealed to the wardens to allow him to make yet another model. Evidently impressed by Antonio, they assented.

Once again the carpenter went to work, this time producing a model that was an even closer replica of Filippo's. This model was none the less rejected by the wardens, at which point the *capomaestro* reputedly told them, '*Fategliene fare un altro e fara el mio*' — that is, 'Let him make another and he will make mine'. Thereafter the relationship between the two former collaborators deteriorated, culminating (as Filippo's battles so often did) with an exchange of insulting sonnets. The episode evidently erased from Filippo's memory his earlier vow to forgive injuries and lay down all hatred. Alas, the lines of wit and vitriol inspired by this conflict have long since been lost to the world. It is sadly ironic that although Filippo's plan prevailed, it was Antonio who had the last laugh: in 1452 he would become *capomaestro* of Santa Maria del Fiore, overseeing the construction of the lantern, complete with a number of his own alterations.

Octagonal in shape, the lantern sits on a marble platform supported by the sandstone chain. Its eight buttresses rise in line with the eight ribs of the dome to support 30-foot-high pilasters crowned with Corinthian capitals. Between the pilasters are eight windows, each also 30 feet in height. The interior features a small dome above which a spire rises 23 feet to be topped by the bronze ball and a cross. Inside one of the buttresses (all of which are hollow in order to decrease the weight of the lantern) a stairway leads to a series of ladders which in turn lead up through the spire and into the bronze ball itself. This giant ball is fitted with a small flap-window that, at 350 feet above the streets, offers Florence's loftiest panorama.

In all, over a million pounds of stone would need to be raised to the top of the cupola. Since the cathedral was now in use, it was impossible to have a large hoist at ground level. This meant the hoist had to be manually operated from the working level and, therefore, small in scale — small enough, that is, for several men to operate in the limited space at the top of the dome. Yet it also had to be capable of raising marble blocks weighing as much as two tons.

Only a few days after the cupola was consecrated, the Opera had announced yet another competition, calling for models of machines 'for hauling loads up on the great cupola'. Filippo, as usual, rose to the challenge. After building a model for a new hoist he was promptly granted the commission along with a prize of 100 florins, the same amount with which he had been rewarded for his design for the ox-hoist many years earlier. Work on this new machine began in the summer of 1442 and was completed the following year.

This new hoist was later sketched by Lorenzo Ghiberti's grandson Buonaccorso. A slightly less complex machine than the ox-hoist, it is nevertheless ingenious in design, featuring multiple pulleys, a counter-weight and a braking system. Buonaccorso's sketch includes a text written in cipher, albeit a fairly crude one. His code (known as the 'Caesar Alphabet' because of the fact that Julius Caesar reputedly invented it) simply replaces each letter in the alphabet with the one that precedes it: B with A, D with C, and so forth. Once decrypted, the text describes the operations of the machine's various parts. In keeping with his nature, Filippo had probably also attempted to guard the secrets of the hoist, especially after his experience with Antonio di Ciaccheri.

The most interesting of the hoist's features was its braking system. Since the men powering the hoist would clearly not have the strength and endurance of the oxen that had driven Filippo's earlier hoist, it was necessary to design a system whereby both the load and counterweight could be suspended in mid-air if necessary. The vertical gear was therefore fitted with a ratchet wheel and a pawl that allowed the load to be locked into position. The gears were also much smaller than those in the ox-hoist, entailing a slower ascent for each payload.

Work on the lantern was delayed because of a familiar problem: the difficulty of acquiring sufficient quantities of *bianchi marmi*. Quarries were

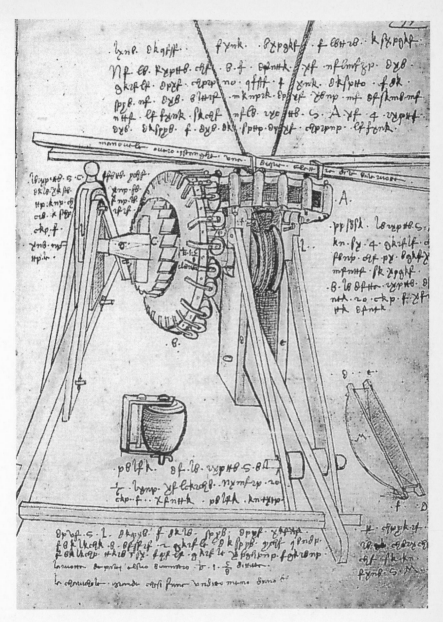

22. Buonaccorso Ghiberti's sketch of Filippo's lantern hoist.

examined near Campiglia as well as at Carrara, but the former proved inadequate because the town of Campiglia failed to provide Filippo's masons with working facilities. In the end, marble did not begin arriving from Carrara until the summer of 1443. It was brought to Florence by sea, river and road. Fifteen years after the wreck of *Il Badalone*, Filippo, now sixty-six, appears to have washed his hands of this particular problem and it was left to Antonio di Ciaccheri to design and build a special cart to carry the marble from Signa to Florence. But Filippo did ensure that, once on the building site, the blocks of marble were protected from the bumps and scrapes of the new hoist by special wooden coverings.

Over the next few years the Piazza del Duomo became so crowded with these blocks of marble – some of which weighed more than 5,000 pounds – that the people of Florence became alarmed at the thought of them stacked on the top of the cupola. Surely it was tempting fate to burden it with so massive a weight? Filippo dismissed these fears, claiming that, far from causing the dome to collapse, the lantern would actually strengthen it by acting as a common keystone for each of the four arches comprising the vault.

Once the blocks of marble had been hoisted to the top of the cupola, they needed to be laid in their places, an operation requiring yet another machine. Construction of a crane for this purpose was begun in 1445. Some 20 feet high and 20 feet wide, this apparatus could not have been raised through the oculus, which was less than 19 feet in diameter; it therefore had to be constructed at the top of the cupola. Walnut logs, pine beams and bronze pins used to build the crane were all winched into the air and then assembled at the dome's summit. Although built under the direction of Antonio di Ciaccheri, who was making himself more and more indispensable to the Opera, the crane was, like all of the other machines used on the dome, the product of Filippo's ingenuity.

As the lantern took shape it became clear that it was an aesthetic triumph. Most later lanterns, including the one built for St Peter's in Rome, would be based on its style. But it also left a more unexpected legacy.

Architectural marvels like Filippo's dome often become sites of scientific inquiry because their unique structures and dimensions can serve as testing grounds for new theories and technologies. Galileo would drop cannonballs from the Leaning Tower of Pisa in order to provide an ocular demonstration that all falling bodies descend with equal velocity independent of weight. Hundreds of years later Gustave Eiffel studied aerodynamics from the top of his tower (where wind speeds regularly reach well over 100 miles per hour) and ultimately proved that the suction over the upper surface of an aeroplane's wing is more important to its flying ability than the air pressure beneath. The dome of Santa Maria del Fiore likewise aided scientific study, only in this case the knowledge gained was used, not for transport through the air but, rather, across the ocean.

Paolo Toscanelli was one of the greatest mathematicians and astronomers of the century. It appears that he met Filippo in about 1425, and he would later call his friendship with the *capomaestro* the greatest association of his life. Like Filippo, Toscanelli was a lifelong bachelor and an unlovely physical specimen, with thick lips, a hooked nose and a weak chin. Although a wealthy man, he forsook all luxury and lived like a monk, sleeping on a wooden plank beside his work table and following a vegetarian diet. He had trained as a physician in Padua but spent most of his time gazing at the heavens and performing complex mathematical calculations. He instructed Filippo in the geometry of Euclid, and later the *capomaestro* would repay the favour, albeit unwittingly, by assisting him with his celestial observations. For in 1475, inspired by the height of the dome, Toscanelli climbed to the top and, with the blessing of the Opera del Duomo, placed a bronze plate at the base of the lantern. This was designed so that the rays of the sun would pass through an aperture in its centre and fall some 300 feet to a special gauge on the floor of the cathedral, a stone inlaid in the Chapel of the Cross. Santa Maria del Fiore was thus transformed into a giant sundial.

This instrument would prove vital to the history of astronomy. The height and stability of the dome allowed Toscanelli to gain a superior knowledge of the sun's motions (or rather the earth's orbit around the sun), which in turn enabled him to calculate with a much greater accuracy than anyone previously the exact moment of both the summer solstice and the vernal equinox. These calculations served an ecclesiastical purpose in that religious dates such as Easter could be carefully regulated, but they also had more far-reaching applications.

After Prince Henry the Navigator founded his school for mariners at Sagres in 1419, the Portuguese had undertaken a number of voyages of discovery in the eastern Atlantic, using a new type of vessel called the caravel, a light, swift ship designed to sail into the wind. The fruits of these voyages were manifold. Portuguese navigators sponsored by Prince Henry had explored the two remotest islands in the Azores (first discovered in 1427) and traced much of the coast of West Africa. The Cape Verde archipelago was sighted off the coast of Africa in 1456 and, fifteen years later, Portuguese sailors crossed the Equator for the first time. But larger prizes still lurked over the horizon. Islands such as Brasil, Antillia and Zacton all existed in legend, but no one had yet set eyes on them. The latter of these islands was said to be especially rich in spices.

These voyages into the Atlantic could not have been made without the aid of astronomy, which permitted mariners to navigate uncharted waters and then make maps of their discoveries. Navigation in a relatively small body of water like the Mediterranean was done by means of charts showing a scale of distances and a pattern of twelve rhumb lines (later expanded to sixteen) that radiated from a central point known as the wind rose. The navigator would simply trace a line between two points, then find the corresponding rhumb line — one running north-north-east, for example — and shape his course from it with the help of a magnetic compass. Questions of longitude and latitude could safely be ignored. But when Portuguese seamen ventured south into the uncharted waters along the west coast of Africa they discovered that this simple method was no longer applicable. The great age of celestial navigation was about to begin.

Crucial to this type of navigation was the astrolabe, an instrument that astronomers used to calculate the position of the sun and other stars with respect to the horizon. By the middle of the 1400s it was being used by mariners to calculate their positions on the ocean. As astronomical determinations of longitude were unreliable, accurate readings of north–south distances — determinations of latitude — were of great importance in both navigation and mapmaking. Mariners calculated their latitude by using the astrolabe to take angle sights on the Pole Star, measuring the angle between its direction overhead and the horizon. As they sailed closer to the Equator, however, the Pole Star sank lower in the sky and this method became impractical. The sun was therefore used instead, the astrolabe measuring its angle above the horizon at midday.

This determination was a simple enough operation except for the fact that the position of the sun, like that of the Pole Star, does not coincide with the celestial pole. In other words, neither of these guides to celestial navigation lies directly on the imaginary extension of the Earth's axis from the North Pole. In order to obtain the latitude of an area it was therefore necessary to apply a correction to their observed altitudes. A number of tables of declination already compiled by astronomers were used for this purpose, most notably the Alfonsine Tables, which had been prepared by Jewish astronomers in Spain in 1252. These tables enabled astronomers and navigators to calculate the positions of the sun and the Pole Star throughout the various seasons, as well as lunar or solar eclipses and the coordinates of any of the planets at any given moment. Two centuries after they were compiled, these tables still contained various inaccuracies and were in need of revision. Toscanelli's observations of the motions of the sun — observations made with the help of the brass plate at the top of Santa Maria del Fiore — led him to correct and refine the Alfonsine Tables, and in doing so he put in the hands of mariners and mapmakers a more accurate tool for plotting their positions.

Toscanelli himself had a particular interest in maps and explorations. In 1459 he interviewed a number of Portuguese sailors familiar with India and the west coast of Africa so that he could create a new and more accurate map of the world. This map then seems to have given rise, in Toscanelli's acute mind, to a novel and striking idea. Fifteen years later, when he was seventy-seven years old, he wrote to a friend in Lisbon, Fernão Martines, a canon at the court of King Afonso of Portugal. He urged Martines to interest Afonso in a sea route to India, assuring him that the Atlantic Ocean was the shortest road to the spice regions of the Orient – a shorter road, that is, than the overland passage normally taken by merchants. Such a route was now necessary because parts of the overland route to India had been closed to Europeans after the Turks captured Constantinople in 1453. Toscanelli therefore appears to have been the first person in history to entertain the idea of sailing west in order to reach India.

King Afonso could not be persuaded to adopt Toscanelli's plan. Although the nephew of Henry the Navigator, he was more interested in slaughtering Moors than discovering new islands in the middle of the ocean. But seven years later the astronomer was contacted by a relative of Fernão Martines: an ambitious and highly-strung Genoese sea captain named Christopher Columbus. An expert navigator, Columbus had sailed all over the known world, from Greece to Iceland to the Gold Coast of Africa. On his voyage to Africa he had spotted flotsam on the current – the trunks of pine tree, large canes, other pieces of wood – that convinced him of the existence to the west of further unknown lands. When he returned to Portugal he had seen Toscanelli's letter to Martines, which so inspired him that he copied it into the flyleaf of one of his books, a treatise on geography that would later accompany him on all four of his voyages to the New World.

Toscanelli wrote back to Columbus, repeating his convictions about the sea route to India. He even sent Columbus a map in which the distance to China was optimistically calculated as being only 6,500 miles – a gross underestimation, of course, but a figure that gave hope to Columbus, in whose mind the map and the letter found fertile soil. However, Columbus had no better luck than Toscanelli in persuading the Portuguese to undertake the venture, and so in 1486 he petitioned for an audience with representatives of King Ferdinand and Queen Isabella of Spain. The rest, of course, is history. Six years later, on 3 August 1492, after funds had been raised and promises of various honours and titles made to Columbus, the tiny fleet of three ships set sail from Cape Palos, near Cartagena, in the hour before dawn. And although Columbus would later claim, with typical arrogance, that neither maps nor mathematics had been of any use to him, it is to be wondered if Europeans would have landed in the New World quite so early and so easily without the maps and tables that Paolo Toscanelli compiled with the help of his observations taken from the dome of Santa Maria del Fiore.

Ingenii Viri Philippi Brunelleschi

THE FIRST STONE of the dome's lantern was consecrated by
Saint Antoninus, the new Archbishop of Florence, in March 1446.
Filippo barely lived long enough to see the ceremony, for he died
a month later, on 15 April, after what appears to have been a short illness.
He died in the house where he had lived for his entire life with his son and
heir, Buggiano, at his bedside. He was sixty-nine years old and had worked
on the site of Santa Maria del Fiore for over a quarter of a century.

Filippo was the first of the three *capomaestri* to die. Battista d'Antonio
survived him by five years. By this time Battista was comfortable and well-
to-do, able to provide fine jewellery for his wife, a dowry for his daughter
and a house for himself in the country. He died at the end of 1451, aged
sixty-seven, after having worked on the site of Santa Maria del Fiore for
his entire adult life.

Lorenzo Ghiberti was to live to the ripe old age of seventy-seven. In
1447, a year after Filippo's death, he completed the ten scenes that make
up his great masterpiece, the 'Doors of Paradise', though the framing and
gilding of these bronze doors would not be finished for another five years.
He had become a wealthy man, with vast lands and several houses,
including a large villa in the country, and his foundry employed as many as
twenty-five apprentices. When he died in December 1455 he was the most

influential sculptor of his age, and it is not altogether without justification that he boasts in his autobiography that very few important works of art executed in Florence had not been devised by his hand.

According to Vasari, the sudden death of Filippo brought tremendous grief to the people of Florence, who appreciated him more in death than they had in life. Even his enemies and rivals were said to have mourned him. But unlike Michelangelo, who would die before the dome of St Peter's was finished, Filippo had at least lived long enough to see his great cupola (with the exception of its lantern) brought to completion.

Funeral obsequies were held in Santa Maria del Fiore. Surrounded by candles and swathed in white muslin, Filippo reposed beneath the great vault that he had finished building a decade earlier. Thousands of mourners paraded past, including the wardens of the Opera, the Wool consuls and masons from the cathedral. Then the candles were snuffed and the body was removed to the campanile, where it would remain for another month while a dispute ensued regarding where the *capomaestro* should be buried. This dispute suggests that Vasari exaggerates when he claims that even Filippo's enemies were in mourning. The delay was probably caused by an anti-Brunelleschi faction who did not wish to see him buried in style, perhaps the same men responsible for jailing him a dozen years earlier. Even in death Filippo was the subject of controversy.*

His supporters eventually won the day. The Signoria decreed that instead of being placed inside his family's sepulchre in the newly rebuilt church of San Marco, where both of his parents were buried, he should have the honour of being entombed inside the cathedral itself, rather like a Pharaoh buried inside a pyramid he had spent his lifetime constructing. He was duly laid to rest in the cathedral on 15 May 1446. There is a fine

---

* This concern for where the bones of such a distinguished citizen of Florence should be laid to rest prefigures how, over a century later, the corpse of Michelangelo would be smuggled back to Florence in a bale of wool after the great sculptor died in Rome. Michelangelo's saintliness is stressed by his friend Vasari, who relates the 'miracle' of how the corpse showed no signs of putrefaction twenty-five days after death, when it was finally buried in Santa Croce.

irony to the fact that, although Filippo did not achieve his ambition of building round the cathedral a series of chapels to house the bones of Florence's wealthiest citizens, he himself should have come to be buried there. This was indeed a great honour. The only other person interred inside the cathedral was Saint Zenobius. His ancient remains had been placed there only a few years earlier in a vault specially built by Filippo.

The *capomaestro* was not laid to rest in a special chapel, however, but in a tomb under the south aisle, near to where Neri di Fioravanti's tantalising model had stood enshrined for so many years. So modest was this tomb (perhaps at the behest of his enemies) that it was only rediscovered during archaeological work on the cathedral in 1972. There is no grand monument to the *capomaestro*, only a simple marble tomb slab – the sort of slab that was cut up for use on the dome whenever marble was scarce. The inscription reads,

CORPUS MAGNI INGENII VIRI PHILIPPI BRUNELLESCHI FIORENTINI

('Here lies the body of the great ingenious man Filippo Brunelleschi of Florence.')

It refers to him, therefore, not directly as an architect but as a man of mechanical genius, alluding to the machines he invented in order to raise the dome.* His mechanical ingenuity is also stressed in the epitaph composed by the Chancellor of Florence, Carlo Marsuppini, a renowned poet, and placed elsewhere in the cathedral. A plan was afoot shortly after his death to decorate the site of his tomb with marble plaques showing some of these machines – an exercise that would have taught us much about their design – but the commission, regrettably, was never carried out.

In 1972 Filippo's bones were exhumed from where, for over five hundred years, they had lain beneath the simple tomb slab. By then the

---

* The words 'genius' and 'ingenious' are etymologically related to ones that describe the building of machines. In medieval Latin the word for machine was *ingenium*, and an *ingeniator* was someone who built them, generally for military purposes.

skeleton had all but crumbled to dust, poignantly illustrating their stark contrast with the mighty vault looming overhead. Forensic tests none the less discovered that, true to contemporary accounts, Filippo was short in stature (no more than 5 feet 4 inches) even by the standards of the fifteenth century. He possessed, however, an above-average cranial capacity. We know what he looked like because shortly after his death the Opera commissioned from Buggiano a plaster cast of his head and shoulders. This bust with its closed eyes and grimacing mouth is now on display in the Museo dell'Opera del Duomo, where visitors can come face to face with the *capomaestro*, who looks barely larger than a child. The Opera also commissioned a marble bust, once again from Buggiano, who portrayed Filippo in the attire of an Ancient Roman. It was placed to the right of the cathedral's door, near to one of Arnolfo di Cambio, with whom the great adventure of the cathedral had begun exactly a century and a half earlier.

These official tributes may strike us as somewhat modest in light of all that Filippo accomplished, but it is safe to assume that no European architect or engineer had ever before earned such renown either during his lifetime or in the years after his death. Today we are so used to celebrating the brilliance of architects like Michelangelo, Andrea Palladio and Sir Christopher Wren that it is hard to imagine a time when architects and architecture were not esteemed. But the great architects of the Middle Ages had been virtually anonymous. The name of the master mason who constructed the abbey of St Denis – the first building ever raised in the Gothic style – remains unrecorded, and the three masons responsible for the ill-fated cathedral at Beauvais are known in the documents simply as the First Master, the Second Master and the Third Master. A little more is known about Arnolfo di Cambio and Neri di Fioravanti, though history does not record where or when either of them was born or died, nor do we have any indication of their personalities or aspirations.

Part of the reason for this anonymity was a prejudice against manual labour on the part of both ancient and medieval authors, who assigned

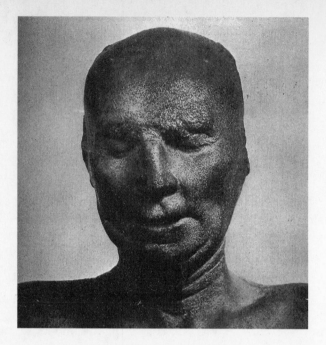

23. Brunelleschi's death mask.

architecture a low place in human achievement, regarding it as an occupation unfit for an educated man. Cicero claimed that architecture was a manual art on the same level as farming, tailoring and metalworking, while in his *Moral Letters* Seneca mired it in the lowest of the four categories of art, those which he classified as *volgares et sordidae* ('common and low'). Such arts were mere handiwork, he claimed, and had no pretence to beauty or honour. As such, architecture ranked even lower than the 'arts of amusement', which included such things as fashioning machinery for stage plays.[1]

Filippo's work at Santa Maria del Fiore set architects on a different path and gave them a new social and intellectual esteem. Largely through his looming reputation, the profession was transformed during the Renaissance from a mechanical into a liberal art, from an art that was viewed as 'common and low' to one that could be regarded as a noble occupation at the heart of the cultural endeavour. Unlike the builders of the Middle Ages, Filippo was far from anonymous, and his feat in raising the dome without a wooden centring was celebrated far and wide. Latin poems were composed in his honour, books were dedicated to him, biographies written, busts carved and portraits painted. He became the subject of myth.

Above all else, Filippo was praised for his *ingegno*, or 'genius', a term invented by the Italian humanist philosophers to describe a natural ability for original invention.[2] Before Filippo's time the faculty of genius was never attributed to architects (or to sculptors and painters either, for that matter).[3] But Marsuppini's epitaph refers to Filippo as possessing *divino ingenio* ('divine genius'), marking the first recorded instance of an architect or sculptor being said to have received divine inspiration for his work. For Vasari, the *capomaestro* had been a genius sent from heaven to renew the moribund art of architecture, almost paralleling how Christ had come to earth to redeem mankind. Yet Filippo was neither a god nor an angel, but only a man, and in his unquestionable brilliance the writers of the Renaissance found their proof that modern man was as great as – and could in fact surpass – the ancients from whom they took their inspiration.

The Nest of Delights

ACH MORNING THE masons working on the dome of Santa
Maria del Fiore arrived on the site in semi-darkness and, after
having their names recorded on the gesso-board, started their
labours by climbing several hundred stone steps to the working level.
Their feet would rasp on the sandstone treads as they began this familiar
but arduous ascent clutching their tools, flasks of wine and the leather
pouches that held their lunches. Their climb through the core of the
building was illuminated by a system of lighting that Filippo – mindful as
ever of his workmen's safety – devised to prevent them from stumbling
and falling in the dark stairwell.[1]

In all, four sets of stairs rise from the ground to the top of the tambour.
A staircase giving access to the top of the drum, and from there into the
dome itself, was built into each of the four enormous piers on which the
dome rests. During construction, two of these were used for ascent and the
other two for descent, thereby doing away with the problem of tool-laden
masons bumping into one another in the confined spaces. The men clearly
needed a good level of fitness to keep their jobs since by the 1430s they
were forced to scale the equivalent of a forty-storey building before
starting work each day.

Originally it was feared that these four stairwells might weaken the piers, obviously a disastrous result considering that they take the bulk of the dome's weight, which has been estimated at 37,000 tons.[2] In the 1380s a group of master masons had recommended bricking up the stairwells and finding another way for the labourers to reach the working levels. But these fears proved unfounded and, thankfully, no such work was ever done. Today it is therefore still possible to follow in the steps of the masons who scaled the heights of the dome.

There are now 463 steps to the summit. Tourists begin their climb in the southwestern pier, passing first through the Porta dei Canonici and then through a much smaller door bearing an *agnus dei*, the emblem of the Wool Guild. The first 150 steps lead to the top of this pier, spiralling anticlockwise and thus allowing for a clockwise descent, which the masons, weary after a day's work, would have found less disorienting. It was these 150 steps that in 1418 defeated the *capomaestro* Giovanni d'Ambrogio, with whom every panting tourist can sympathise: he was sacked for being unable to climb them in order to inspect the workmanship.

The steps through the southwestern pier eventually lead on to an interior balcony that encircles the base of the dome. It was at this height that the masons held their small feast of bread and melons in the summer of 1420. From this vantage point they must have realised the magnitude of the task before them, because nowhere does the span of the dome seem greater than here, where you can gaze across the huge, echoing void. The vast interior of the vault that soars overhead is now decorated by one of the world's largest frescoes, Vasari's *Last Judgement*, with its gesticulating skeletons and gargantuan, pitchfork-wielding demons.[3] Filippo anticipated the execution of this fresco, and iron rings from which scaffolding could be hung were inserted into the interior of the inner shell. The shell is also pierced by small windows through which a painter could crawl on to the hanging platform and begin work with his brushes.

From the interior balcony a small door leads into the gradually narrowing space between the two shells, where another set of steps threads its way upwards. These steps were constructed at the same time as the cupola itself. Still remarkably unworn after more than five centuries of use, they were built out of sandstone beams delivered from the Trassinaia quarry. To the right of the staircase, sloping gently inwards, is the plastered surface of the inner dome, while the outer shell runs overhead in a parallel arc. In between these two tilting walls is a disorienting maze of low doorways, cramped passageways and irregularly ascending staircases that make the ascent a little like stepping into an Escher lithograph. It seems ironic that the first building built in the 'Renaissance style' – this dome that is outwardly so ordered and graceful – should have at its core such a bewildering labyrinth of musty corridors.

It is in this confusing and constricted space between the two domes that you can see at close hand the techniques used by Filippo and his masons. In the places where the plaster on the inner dome has fallen away the herring-bone pattern is exposed to view, its elongated bricks rubbed smooth as glass by many thousand passing hands. In other places the transverse beams of the stone chains can be seen crossing overhead like thick rafters. Part of the wooden chain is visible too. Its timbers are low enough for the present-day visitor to touch, though the original chestnut beams were replaced during the eighteenth century after they began to rot.

One of the most striking features of the climb is the series of small round windows that pierce the outer shell like portholes. These apertures bring light and air into the passages of dank stone, and through them you catch brief glimpses of the higgledy-piggledy rooftops of Florence as they recede ever further below. These windows, of which there are seventy-two in all, form part of Filippo's method of windproofing the dome, an attempt to protect the structure from high winds in the same way that damage to houses from tornadoes can be limited by opening their doors and windows. On blustery days the wind can be heard whistling through their openings.

A final set of steps (above which the outer shell has been cut back to allow for more headroom) leads to the octagonal viewing platform at the base of the lantern. It comes as a mild shock, having passed through the echoing, disorienting passages, then suddenly to emerge outdoors, amid wind and light, high above the ground, with a dizzying panorama of

Florence and the surrounding hills at your feet. The buttresses of the lantern loom overhead like marble tree trunks, and from this proximity it is possible to see the immense size of their 5,000-pound blocks, as well as the precision with which the marble has been cut and fitted together. Stepping closer to the edge of the viewing platform you can see the tiled sides of the dome fall dramatically away. And from this spot another advantage of the *quinto acuto* profile becomes evident: the steep rise means you can see almost directly into the piazza below – and, by the same token, most of the dome, including the lantern, is visible at close range from the ground.

Today tourists linger for ten or fifteen minutes on the platform before beginning their descent (some of them carrying the cupola-shaped umbrellas that are sold in Florence's market stalls). They spend their time taking photographs, pointing out familiar landmarks, or even surreptitiously inscribing their initials on the buttresses of the lantern, which are now covered with graffiti. For most of them the climb is a means to an end, an ordeal that must be suffered in order to gain a panoramic view of the city. But centuries ago this long ascent was made by a somewhat more interested party. In the late 1540s, after being named architect-in-chief of St Peter's, Michelangelo, by then an old man, was given three passes into the cupola so that he and two of his assistants could inspect Filippo's methods of construction before beginning work on the drum and dome of St Peter's. A proud Florentine, Michelangelo claimed that he could equal Filippo's dome but never surpass it. In fact he did not even equal it, for the cupola of St Peter's, completed in 1590, is almost ten feet narrower and, arguably, much less graceful and striking.

Indeed, in height and span the cupola of Santa Maria del Fiore has never really been surpassed. Sir Christopher Wren's cupola for St Paul's Cathedral in London, with a diameter of 112 feet, is smaller by thirty feet, and a more recent dome, that of the Capitol in Washington DC, is only 95 feet in span, less than two-thirds the size of the one in Florence. Not until the twentieth century were wider vaults raised, and then only by using modern materials like plastic, high-carbon steel and aluminum, which have permitted the construction of vast tent-like structures such as the Astrodome in Houston, Texas, or the lightweight, prefabricated geodesic domes of Buckminster Fuller. Even so, it is no coincidence that, like Michelangelo, the master of large-scale concrete vaulting in the twentieth century, Pier Luigi Nervi, made a technical examination of Santa Maria del Fiore in the 1930s before developing the vaulting techniques he used in structures such as the Vatican audience hall and the Palazzo dello Sport in Rome. It seems wholly appropriate that this masterpiece executed by Filippo, the 'treasure hunter' who once surveyed the ruins of Rome, should have become an object of study by the generations of architects who followed him.

The effect of the dome has been eloquently described by Alberti in *Della tranquillità dell'animo*, his dialogue on the tranquillity of the soul. Here he has the disillusioned politician Agnolo Pandolfini – the man who finds solace for his troubled mind in fantasies about gigantic hoists and cranes – compare the state of spiritual calm to the peaceful interior of Santa Maria del Fiore, through which he strolls with his companion Nicola de' Medici, the failed banker. For Agnolo, the cathedral is an example of grace under pressure, of an ability to withstand the blows of fortune that he compares to adverse weather conditions that buffet the walls of the building but leave the beautiful interior pacific and unruffled:

> *Within, one breathes the perpetual freshness of spring. Outside there may be frost, fog or wind, but in this retreat, closed to every wind, the air is quiet and mild. What a pleasant refuge from the hot blasts of summer and autumn! And if it is true that delight resides where our senses receive all that they can demand of nature, how can one hestitate to call this temple a nest of delights?*

Yet, for all its grandeur, the cathedral and its dome have not been as impervious to the elements and other outside forces as Agnolo suggests. Vasari was to claim that the heavens themselves are envious of the dome since every day it is struck by lightning, and over the years a number of these strikes have caused serious damage. No means of countering lightning existed at the time, and a system of lightning rods was not introduced at the cathedral until the second half of the nineteenth century, by which time the lantern had needed major repairs on several occasions.* The most dramatic of these blows fell on 5 April 1492, when a lightning bolt sent several tons of marble cascading into the streets on the north side of the cupola, in the direction of the Villa Careggi, which stands in the hills above Florence. The Villa Careggi was the country home of Lorenzo de' Medici, the grandson of Cosimo de' Medici and, like Cosimo, the ruler of Florence and a generous patron of the arts. To Lorenzo, lying ill with a fever in the villa, the meaning of the destructive strike was unmistakable: 'I am a dead man!' he exclaimed upon being told in which direction the rubble had fallen. Lorenzo's physicians attempted to avert this fate, feeding him potions made from pulverised diamonds and pearls, and cautioning him to avoid both grape pips and the air at sunset, two things considered fatal to a man in his condition. But they laboured in vain, and true to his prediction Lorenzo died three days later, on Passion Sunday.

In 1639 a series of cracks appeared on the interior of the inner shell. These are similar to those that appeared at almost the same time in the dome of St Peter's. They run vertically from the oculus to the drum, cutting through Vasari's fresco and in many places following the line of the herring-bone bond. The causes of these fissures, as well as the remedial measures they call for, have been matters of debate ever since. Sophisticated thermal measuring devices have been inserted into a series of holes bored in the inner dome in order to monitor the cracks, and in 1970 Rowland Mainstone suggested as their probable cause the expansion of the iron rods in the iron-and-sandstone chains. This increase in size was the result, he claimed, of both temperature changes and the penetration of the masonry by moisture which was causing the iron to rust. He found that the cracks were not, like those in the dome of St Peter's, the result of an inherent structural deficiency given that the

---

* The Ancient Romans had a dubious method of protecting their buildings from lightning: believing that eagles and sea-calves were never struck, they buried the corpses of these creatures within the walls in the hope of warding off disaster.

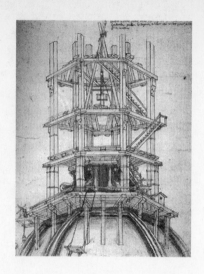

24. & 25. The lantern being struck by lightning in 1601 – and
the scaffolding erected to repair it.

materials used were able to withstand the stresses generated by the cupola.[4]
Another cause might be the cathedral's alarmingly poor foundations: in the
1970s a hydrologist discovered that a subterranean stream flows under the
southwest corner of the dome, directly beneath the pier in whose staircase
tourists now begin their ascent. The massive cupola was raised, in other
words, on top of an underground river.

Shortly after Mainstone's analysis, a commission appointed by the
Italian government reported, to widespread alarm, that the cracks in the
dome were growing in both length and breadth. This claim had been
dramatically illustrated a few months earlier by the fall of a large fragment
of Vasari's fresco. The worsening situation was blamed on a violent form
of stress that Filippo, for all his genius, could not have anticipated: heavy
traffic. Cars and buses were immediately banned from the area around the
cathedral, and today only refuse lorries on their early-morning rounds are
permitted to trundle through the Piazza del Duomo. Filippo's dome, so

long impervious to the harsh vagaries of the weather, is now also safe from the scourge of the motor car.

Today, as for the past five centuries, the mountainous form of the cupola dominates Florence. It looms above the narrow streets as you walk them, or breaks unexpectedly into view whenever you turn a corner or enter a piazza. It can be seen from the steps of churches such as San Miniato al Monte, from hotel balconies (as Lucy Honeychurch discovers in E. M. Forster's *A Room With a View*) and from the terraces of cafés. On clear days it is even visible from as far away as Pistoia, fifteen miles to the west, where in the fifteenth century the citizens renamed one of their streets the Via dell'Apparenza, the 'Street of the Appearance', as if the dome were not simply brick, stone and marble, the result of a remarkable feat of structural engineering, but instead a miraculous apparition, the handiwork of God or his angels that had materialised overnight in the Arno Valley like the fresco in the convent of Santissima Annunziata that the Florentines believed was painted by an angel. And there is indeed something miraculous about the sight of the dome regardless of where it is viewed from, whether close up or far away. The fact that it was built by men — and built amid war and intrigue, with only a limited understanding of the forces of nature — only makes it more of a wonder.

Notes

1 See Franklin K. B. Toker, 'Florence Cathedral: The Design Stage', *Art Bulletin* 60 (1978), pp. 226–7.

2 Although the precise details of his role in the design of the cupola are not known for certain, Neri is constantly identified in the documents as the leader of the committee: the 1367 project is defined as *facto per Nerium Fioravantis et alios magistros et pictores* ('done by Neri di Fioravanti and other masters and painters'). Other members of the committee included Taddeo Gaddi, formerly one of Giotto's assistants; Andrea Orcagna, a pupil of Andrea Pisano and the most pre-eminent artist in Florence following the death of Giotto; and Orcagna's brother, Benci di Cione.

3 Much later the Spanish architect Antonio Gaudí would refer to the flying buttresses of Gothic cathedrals as unfortunate 'crutches'. He sought to design structures that would channel the lateral thrusts to the ground more directly. See Jack Zunz, 'Working on the Edge: The Engineer's Dilemma', in R. J. W. Milne, ed., *Structural Engineering: History and Development* (London: E. & F. N. Spon, 1997), p. 62.

4 The exact dating of the plan for the tambour is difficult to determine, as is its original designer. Giorgio Vasari, not always reliable, attributes its design to Brunelleschi: see *Lives of the Artists*, 2 vols, ed. and trans. George Bull (Harmondsworth, Middlesex: Penguin, 1987), vol. 1, p. 141. This argument is accepted in Carlo Guasti, *La cupola di Santa Maria del Fiore* (Florence, 1857), pp. 189–90, and Frank D. Prager and Gustina Scaglia, *Brunelleschi: Studies of his Technology and Inventions* (Cambridge, Mass.: MIT Press, 1971) pp. 18–22. Other scholars date the plans for the project much earlier, attributing them variously to Arnolfo di Cambio, Giovanni di Lapo Ghini, or Andrea Orcagna. See A. Nardini-Despotti-Mospignotti, *Filippo Brunelleschi e la cupola* (Florence, 1885), p. 97; E. von Stegmann and H. von Geymüller, *Die Architektur der Renaissance in der Toskana* (Munich, 1885–93), pp. 38ff; and Howard Saalman, *Filippo Brunelleschi: The Cupola of Santa Maria del Fiore* (London: A. Zwemmer, 1980), p. 48.

5 The dome of San Vitale in Ravenna, built in the sixth century AD, consists of a double shell. Closer to home, the Baptistery of San Giovanni in Florence is

technically a double dome in that it features an octagonal vault surmounted by a pyramidal wooden roof. It is usually assumed that the Baptistery is the prototype for the dome of Santa Maria del Fiore. After the cupola of Santa Maria del Fiore was built, it would become a standard feature of domes in Europe, including St Peter's in Rome. Sir Christopher Wren's design for St Paul's in London would even call for three domes, one inside the other.

2: THE GOLDSMITH OF SAN GIOVANNI

1 For Brunelleschi's career as a clockmaker, see Frank D. Prager, 'Brunelleschi's Clock?' *Physis* 10 (1963), pp. 203–16.

2 A point made by Frederick Hartt in 'Art and Freedom in Quattrocento Florence', in *Essays in Memory of Karl Lehmann*, ed. Lucy Freeman Sandler (New York: Institute of Fine Arts, 1964), p. 124.

3 See Richard Krautheimer, *Lorenzo Ghiberti* (Princeton: Princeton University Press, 1956), p. 3.

3: THE TREASURE HUNTERS

1 For the classic statement of this connection, see Hans Baron, *The Crisis of the Early Italian Renaissance: Civic Humanism and Republican Liberty in an Age of Classicism and Tyranny* (Princeton: Princeton University Press, 1955).

2 This ordinance had ordered Florence's merchants to employ the more cumbersome Roman numerals instead of Arabic ones, whose shapes had not yet been standardised, therefore giving rise, potentially, to confusion and error. Resistance to Arabic notation was common in Europe during the Middle Ages. See David M. Burton, *Burton's History of Mathematics* (Dubuque, Iowa: William C. Brown, 1995), p. 255.

3 Filippo's reputation as the revivalist of Roman architecture – a reputation established by Manetti and Vasari – has lately come under scrutiny from a number of scholars who argue that his architectural vocabulary (pediments, semicircular arches, fluted pilasters, Corinthian capitals) could actually have been acquired much closer to home, and from buildings of a more recent date. See, for example, Howard Saalman, 'Filippo Brunelleschi: Capital Studies', *Art Bulletin* 40 (1959), pp. 115ff; Howard Burns, 'Quattrocento Architecture and the Antique: Some Problems', in R. R. Bolgar, ed., *Classical Influences on European Culture* (Cambridge: Cambridge University Press, 1971), pp. 269–87; and John

Onians, *Bearers of Meaning: The Classical Orders in Antiquity, the Middle Ages and the Renaissance* (Cambridge: Cambridge University Press, 1988), pp. 130-6. Onians argues, for instance, that Filippo participated in a 'Tuscan Renaissance' as opposed to a Roman one: Filippo saw his task 'as essentially to purify and regularise the primitive Tuscan architecture which was best represented in the Baptistery' (p. 136). Onians even dismisses Filippo's visit to Rome as an invention of Manetti. But for evidence of this sojourn, see Diane Finiello Zervas, 'Filippo Brunelleschi's Political Career', *Burlington Magazine* 121 (October 1979), p. 633. A case for Filippo's study of Roman remains – particularly their structural details – is also made by Rowland Mainstone. See 'Brunelleschi's Dome of S. Maria del Fiore and some Related Structures', *Transactions of the Newcomen Society* 42 (1969–70), p. 123; and 'Brunelleschi's Dome', *Architectural Review* (September 1977), pp. 164–6.

4: AN ASS AND A BABBLER

1 See Martin Kemp, 'Science, Non-science and Nonsense: The Interpretation of Brunelleschi's Perspective', *Art History* (June 1978), pp. 143–5; and Jehane R. Kuhn, 'Measured Appearances: Documentation and Design in Early Perspective Drawing', *Journal of the Warburg and Courtauld Institutes* 53 (1990), pp. 114–32.
2 Rowland Mainstone, 'Brunelleschi's Dome', p. 159.
3 See, for example, J. Durm, 'Die Domkuppel in Florenz und die Kuppel der Peterskirche in Rom', *Zeitschrift für Bauwesen* (Berlin, 1887), pp. 353–74; Stegmann and Geymüller, *Die Architektur der Renaissance in der Toskana* (Munich, 1885–93); and Paolo Sanpaolesi, *La cupola di Santa Maria del Fiore* (Rome: Reale Istituto d'Archaologia e Storia dell'Arte, 1941).

5: THE RIVALS

1 It has been suggested that Lorenzo, like Filippo, proposed to vault the cupola without armature. See Paolo Sanpaolesi, 'Il concorso del 1418–20 per la cupole di S. Maria del Fiore', *Rivista d'arte* (1936), p. 330. But no evidence supports this claim. See Krautheimer, *Lorenzo Ghiberti*, p. 254.
2 The Barbadori Chapel was endowed by Bartolomeo Barbadori, a wealthy wool merchant who died of the plague in 1400. His son Tommaso was serving the Opera del Duomo in 1418. The Ridolfi Chapel was endowed by Schiatta Ridolfi, one of the Wool consuls in 1418.

3 Marvin Trachtenberg, 'Review of Howard Saalman, *Filippo Brunelleschi*', *Journal of the Society of Architectural Historians* 42 (1983), p. 292.

4 For the argument in favour of Filippo's authorship, see Saalman, *Filippo Brunelleschi*, pp. 77–9.

6: MEN WITHOUT NAME OR FAMILY

1 Sanpaolesi, *La cupola di Santa Maria del Fiore*, p. 21.

2 Vincent Cronin, *The Florentine Renaissance* (London: Collins, 1967), p. 96.

3 William Barclay Parsons, *Engineers and Engineering in the Renaissance* (Baltimore: Williams & Wilkins, 1939), p. 589.

7: SOME UNHEARD-OF MACHINE

1 These dimensions have been calculated in Frank D. Prager, 'Brunelleschi's Inventions and the "Renewal of Roman Masonry Work"', *Osiris* 9 (1950), p. 517.

2 Prager, 'Brunelleschi's Inventions', p. 524.

3 Prager, 'Brunelleschi's Inventions', p. 517.

4 Prager and Scaglia, *Brunelleschi: Studies of his Technology and Inventions*, p. 80.

5 See Paul Lawrence Rose, *The Italian Renaissance of Mathematics: Studies in Humanists and Mathematicians from Petrarch to Galileo* (Geneva: Librairie Droz, 1975).

6 On the possible design of Filippo's clock, see Prager, 'Brunelleschi's Clock?', pp. 203–16.

8: THE CHAIN OF STONE

1 Hugh Plommer, ed., *Vitruvius and Later Roman Building Manuals* (Cambridge: Cambridge University Press, 1973), p. 53.

2 John Fitchen notes that many Byzantine churches besides Santa Sophia incorporated wooden ties to reduce the impact of earthquakes. See *The Construction of Gothic Cathedrals: A Study of Medieval Vault Erection* (Oxford: Oxford University Press, 1961), p. 278.

3 Mainstone, 'Brunelleschi's Dome of S. Maria del Fiore', p. 116.

9: THE TALE OF THE FAT CARPENTER

1 The story is printed in Thomas Roscoe, ed., *The Italian Novelists*, 4 vols (London, 1827), vol. 3, pp. 305–24.

10: THE POINTED FIFTH

1 The only source for this story – not related by either Manetti or Vasari – is Giovanni Battista Gelli's account in *Brevi vite di artisti fiorentini*, published during the sixteenth century.

2 Dumas, ed., *A History of Technology and Invention* (London: John Murray, 1980), p. 397.

3 Eugenio Battisti, *Brunelleschi: The Complete Work*, trans. Robert Erich Wolf (London: Thames & Hudson, 1981), p. 361. Several scholars have proposed a different method of curvature control, the so-called *gualandrino con tre corde* mentioned in the 1426 amendments to the cupola programme. This procedure involves a complicated series of triangulations performed with three ropes stretched across the diameter of the cupola. For reconstructions, see Mainstone, 'Brunelleschi's Dome', p. 164, and Saalman, *Filippo Brunelleschi*, pp. 162–4. In fact, however, the *gualandrino* was not a system of curvature control but a safety harness worn by the masons: see Battisti, p. 361.

4 See Howard Saalman, 'Giovanni di Gherardo da Prato's Designs concerning the Cupola of Santa Maria del Fiore in Florence', *Journal of the Society of Architectural Historians* 18 (1950), p. 18.

11: BRICKS AND MORTAR

1 For information on the brick-making industry in Florence, I am indebted to Richard A. Goldthwaite, *The Building of Renaissance Florence: An Economic and Social History* (Baltimore: The Johns Hopkins University Press, 1980), pp. 171–212.

2 Saalman, *Filippo Brunelleschi*, p. 199.

3 Mainstone, 'Brunelleschi's Dome of Santa Maria del Fiore and some Related Structures', p. 114. Mainstone calculates that at this pace there would be 'ample time for each course to become self-supporting before the next was added' (pp. 114–15).

4 Samuel Kline Cohn, Jr., *The Laboring Classes in Renaissance Florence* (New York: Academic Press, 1980), p. 205.

5 *Lives of the Artists*, vol. 1, p. 156.

6 Mainstone, 'Brunelleschi's Dome of S. Maria del Fiore', p. 113.

7 See Robert Field, *Geometrical Patterns from Tiles and Brickwork* (Diss, Norfolk: Tarquin, 1996), pp. 14, 40; and Andrew Plumbridge and Wim Meulenkamp, *Brickwork: Architecture and Design* (London: Studio Vista, 1993), pp. 146–7.

8 See Iris Origo, 'The Domestic Enemy: The Eastern Slaves in Tuscany in the Fourteenth and Fifteenth Centuries', *Speculum: A Journal of Mediaeval Studies* 30 (July 1955), pp. 321–56.

12: CIRCLE BY CIRCLE

1 See Christine Smith, *Architecture in the Culture of Early Humanism: Ethics, Aesthetics and Eloquence, 1400–1470* (Oxford: Oxford University Press, 1992), pp. 40–53.
2 This point is made in Smith, *Architecture in the Culture of Early Humanism*, p. 45.
3 Mainstone, 'Brunelleschi's Dome', p. 163.
4 Mainstone, 'Brunelleschi's Dome', p. 164.
5 See Karl Lehmann, 'The Dome of Heaven', *Art Bulletin* 27 (1945), pp. 1–27; and Abbas Daneshvari, *Medieval Tomb Towers of Iran: An Iconographical Study* (Lexington, Kentucky: Mazdâ Publishers, 1986), pp. 14–16.

13: THE MONSTER OF THE ARNO

1 M. E. Mallett, *Florentine Galleys of the Fifteenth Century* (Oxford: Clarendon Press, 1967), p. 16.
2 See Maximilian Frumkin, 'Early History of Patents for Invention', *Transactions of the Newcomen Society* 26 (1947–9), p. 48.
3 Quoted in Prager and Scaglia, *Brunelleschi*, p. 111.
4 Quoted in Prager and Scaglia, *Brunelleschi*, p. 129.

14: DÉBÂCLE AT LUCCA

1 Prager and Scalia, *Brunelleschi*, p. 131.
2 Quoted in Prager and Scaglia, *Brunelleschi*, p. 129

15: FROM BAD TO WORSE

1 Goldthwaite, *The Building of Renaissance Florence*, p. 257.
2 See Zervas, 'Filippo Brunelleschi's Political Career', pp. 630–9.
3 Battisti, *Filippo Brunelleschi*, p. 42.

18: INGENII VIRI PHILIPPI BRUNELLESCHI

1 *Ad Lucilium Epistulae Morales*, 3 vols, trans. Richard M. Gummere (London: Heinemann, 1920), vol. 2, p. 363.

2 See Christine Smith, *Architecture in the Culture of Early Humanism*, p. 30; and Martin Kemp, 'From *Mimesis* to *Fantasia*: The Quattrocento Vocabulary of Creation, Inspiration and Genius in the Visual Arts', *Viator* 8 (1977), p. 394.

3 For a discussion, see Kemp, 'From *Mimesis* to *Fantasia*', pp. 347–98.

19: THE NEST OF DELIGHTS

1 The details of this system of lighting are not recorded, unfortunately, and so remain a matter of conjecture. But alchemists of the day – inspired by stories from the Roman histories about how a perpetual fire was kindled in the Temple of Vesta in Rome – were interested in flames that would burn continuously. Accordingly, they conducted experiments in which, for example, salt was added to lamp oil to make it burn more slowly. Other experiments – equally unsuccessful – saw wicks made from 'incombustible' stones. For a discussion of these experiments, see Giovanni Battista della Porta, *Natural Magick in XX Books* (London, 1658), p. 303.

2 Paolo Galluzzi, *Mechanical Marvels: Invention in the Age of Leonardo* (Florence: Giunti, 1996), p. 20.

3 The fresco was begun by Vasari in 1572 and completed after his death by Federico Zuccaro (1540–1609). It was restored between 1981 and 1994.

4 Mainstone, 'Brunelleschi's Dome of S. Maria del Fiore and Some Related Structures', pp. 120–1. In 1743 three iron rings needed to be installed in St Peter's in order to prevent the cracked dome from collapsing altogether. The incorporation of these chains is a landmark in the history of structural engineering. Three French mathematicians – Boscovitch, le Seur and Jacquier – calculated the horizontal thrust of the dome as well as the tensile strength of iron and the resistance of the drum walls. Their work represents the first time that statics and structural mechanics were successfully applied to such a problem. For discussions, see Hans Straub, *A History of Civil Engineering*, trans. E. Rockwell (London: L. Hill, 1952), pp. 112–16; and Edoardo Benvenuto, *An Introduction to the History of Structural Mechanics*, 2 vols (New York: Springer-Verlag, 1991), vol. 2, p. 352.

Select Bibliography

Alberti, Leon Battista, *Ten Books on Architecture* (London: A. Tiranti, 1965)

Battisti, Eugenio, *Brunelleschi: The Complete Work* (London: Thames & Hudson, 1981)

Gaertner, Peter, *Brunelleschi* (Cologne: Könemann, 1998)

Galluzzi, Paolo, *Mechanical Marvels: Invention in the Age of Leonardo* (Florence: Giunti, 1996)

Ghiberti, Lorenzo, *The Commentaries*, trans. Julius von Schlosser (London: Courtauld Institute of Art, 1948–67)

Goldthwaite, Richard A., *The Building of Renaissance Florence: An Economic and Social History* (Baltimore: Johns Hopkins University Press, 1980)

Mainstone, Rowland J., 'Brunelleschi's Dome' *Architectural Review* (September 1977), 157–66

Mainstone, Rowland J., 'Brunelleschi's Dome of S. Maria del Fiore and Some Related Structures' *Transactions of the Newcomen Society* 42 (1969–70), 107–26

Mainstone, Rowland J., *Developments in Structural Form* (Cambridge, Mass.: Harvard University Press, 1975)

Manetti, Antonio di Tucci, *The Life of Brunelleschi*, trans. Catherine Enggass (University Park: Pennsylvania State University Press, 1970)

Prager, Frank D., 'Brunelleschi's Clock?' *Physis* 10 (1963), 203–16

Prager, Frank D., 'Brunelleschi's Inventions and the "Renewal of Roman Masonry Work"' *Osiris* 9 (1950), 457–554

Prager, Frank D. and Gustina Scaglia, *Brunelleschi: Studies of his Technology and Inventions* (Cambridge, Mass.: The MIT Press, 1970)

Saalman, Howard, *Filippo Brunelleschi: The Cupola of Santa Maria del Fiore* (London: A. Zwemmer, 1980)

Toker, Franklin K. B., 'Florence Cathedral: The Design Stage' *Art Bulletin* 60 (1978), 214–30

Vasari, Giorgio, *Lives of the Artists*, 2 vols, ed. and trans. George Bull (Harmondsworth, Middlesex: Penguin, 1987)

Index